"*PRAYzing!* is AMAzing! This wonderful book puts in the hands of prayer leaders all the resources needed for creative, powerful prayer meetings. No one ever leaves a Daniel Henderson-led prayer meeting bored, and this book shows why."

—DAVE BUTTS, chairman, America's National Prayer Committee

"Daniel understands what prayer is really all about: worship! And nothing could be more needed in our spiritually starved world today than true worship. Daniel's practical, creative ideas come from hours alone with God. He is a man of great passion—passion for fresh, exciting, and Spirit-led prayer. God is using him to awaken the church and lead us all to our knees. May this book renew our hearts and lead us to spiritual revival so that all the nations can worship Him!"

—VERNON BREWER, president, World Help; author of *The Forgotten Children* and *Why? Answers to Weather the Storms of Life*

"Daniel's passion for prayer is contagious. He understands both the problem with corporate prayer gatherings and the solution! We couldn't wait to finish the book so that we could go out and organize a grand PRAYzing gathering. Any church member who thinks prayer is boring should read this book. Then someday after we try to figure out how our nationwide revival began, we'll track it down to Daniel Henderson! Don't miss out!"

—JIM AND KAREN COVELL, film composers and TV producers; coauthors of *How to Talk About Jesus Without Freaking Out* and *The Day I Met God*

"I had the privilege of being Daniel Henderson's pastor when he surrendered his life to become a preacher. He was then as he is now: deeply serious about his commitment to the Lord. I visited Arcade Church in Sacramento, California, where Daniel was pastor for ten years before moving to Grace Church in Eden Prairie, Minnesota. I found an entire church pulsating with prayer. Daniel has found the secret of turning his churches into houses of prayer, as Jesus suggested. He is truly a doer of the Word and not a hearer only."

—DR. JAMES W. BRYANT, ThD, senior professor of pastoral theology, Criswell College

"Having written several books, spoken all over the world, and founded ministries devoted to prayer, I feel I have given my life to ever-deepening times alone with God. But as I finished chapter 4 of *PRAYzing!*, I had the strange feeling of being drawn up to a higher prayer level, intertwining the Word of God's instructions with worship, praising, repenting, and commitment praying. This book's simple yet incredibly profound prayer strategy inspires the heart, not just the head. No matter where you and I are in our prayer journey, God always has something creative to add. Perhaps here it is, for you."

—EVELYN CHRISTENSON, speaker; author of
What Happens When Women Pray

"After establishing the need for a fresh approach to how we pray, Daniel Henderson offers a veritable A-Z of creative ideas for revitalizing our individual and corporate times of seeking the Lord. I appreciate in particular Daniel's effort to ground his suggestions in Scripture and to share helpful anecdotes interspersed throughout the text to illustrate how those ideas may play out in practice."

—DR. RANDALL ROBERTS, academic dean and professor of
spiritual formation, Western Seminary

"Daniel Henderson is a man of prayer and a pastor who has effectively encouraged and enabled his people to pray. I sincerely recommend this book to every Christian who wants to be more effective in prayer."

—DR. PAUL CEDAR, chairman, Mission America Coalition

"'When more people are attending our weeknight prayer meeting than the Sunday morning worship service, revival will come.' Not only was it a daunting challenge put forth by Reverend McLeod to his congregation in the early 1970s, it was an intensely deliberate one. As a result, that day came. People prayed. Then they worshiped. Then God's people all across Canada were quickened by an amazing work of God's Holy Spirit. Today, in *PRAYzing!*, Daniel Henderson deliberately puts forth the same challenge to every serious Christian. Pray or perish. Seek Him or miss Him. Revival or ruin. This tool is practical. Inspiring. Helpful. And immensely needed. May God use it to draw us near to Himself and Himself near to us, until He deluges us with His manifest presence."

—BYRON PAULUS, president, Life Action Ministries

"If you know in the depths of your heart the value and imperativeness of prayer, yet your experience in group prayer has been tepid at best, *PRAYzing!* will breathe life, vitality, and reality into your experience. And what's more, in the process, your relationship with God will be enriched and energized. Am I promising too much? Try it!"

—DR. PAUL S. HONTZ, senior pastor, Central Wesleyan Church,
Holland, Michigan

PRAYzing!

CREATIVE PRAYER EXPERIENCES FROM A TO Z

DANIEL HENDERSON

NAVPRESS

Discipleship Inside Out®

Discipleship Inside Out®

NavPress is the publishing ministry of The Navigators, an international Christian organization and leader in personal spiritual development. NavPress is committed to helping people grow spiritually and enjoy lives of meaning and hope through personal and group resources that are biblically rooted, culturally relevant, and highly practical.

For a free catalog go to www.NavPress.com or call 1.800.366.7788 in the United States or 1.800.839.4769 in Canada.

ISBN-13: 978-1-60006-189-9

Cover design and illustration: The DesignWorks Group, Jason Gabbert www.thedesignworksgroup.com
Creative Team: Dave Wilson, Susan Miller, Cara Iverson, Darla Hightower, Arvid Wallen, Pat Reinheimer

Some of the anecdotal illustrations in this book are true to life and are included with the permission of the persons involved. All other illustrations are composites of real situations, and any resemblance to people living or dead is coincidental.

Unless otherwise identified, all Scripture quotations in this publication are taken from the *New King James Version* (NKJV). Copyright © 1982 by Thomas Nelson, Inc. Used by permission. All rights reserved. Other versions used include: the *New American Standard Bible* (NASB), © The Lockman Foundation 1960, 1962, 1963, 1968, 1971, 1972, 1973, 1975, 1977, 1995; *THE MESSAGE* (MSG). Copyright © 1993, 1994, 1995, 1996, 2000, 2001, 2002, 2005. Used by permission of NavPress Publishing Group; the *Amplified New Testament* (AMP), © The Lockman Foundation 1954, 1958; and the *Holy Bible, New Living Translation* (NLT), copyright © 1996. Used by permission of Tyndale House Publishers, Inc., Wheaton, Illinois 60189. All rights reserved.

Henderson, Daniel.
 Prayzing! : creative prayer experiences from A to Z / Daniel Henderson.
   p. cm.
 Includes bibliographical references.
 ISBN-13: 978-1-60006-189-9
 ISBN-10: 1-60006-189-3
 1. Prayer--Christianity. 2. Worship. I. Title.
 BV210.3.H465 2007
 248.3'2--dc22
                              2007011120

Printed in the United States of America

4 5 6 7 8 9 10 11 / 18 17 16 15 14 13

To Rosemary, in honor of our
twenty-five years of grace-filled marriage
and priceless memories as partners in life and ministry.
and
To my brother, Dennis S. Henderson,
My childhood hero, lifelong friend, fellow pastor, and
treasured colaborer in the work of renewal.
Thank you for partnering with me in the vision for pastor-
led, local church-oriented movements of Christ-exalting,
worship-based prayer—leading to a full-scale revival, super-
natural evangelism, and cultural transformation.
and
To Pastor Jim Cymbala, whose example of
praying and pastoral leadership has inspired me
to persevere and to discover
countless experiences of PRAYzing!

CONTENTS

FOREWORD

Some books are about theory. Others reflect the reality of practical life experience. This book is pure reality and packed with inspiration that applies to every life and congregation.

When I first read the early chapters of Daniel's book, I was sitting in a doctor's office waiting for some routine blood work. I actually laughed aloud. He describes the story of my life: trying to stay awake while praying. It is a battle we all face and an important issue for every church.

As a minister for over sixty years, I have known the challenge of trying to sustain prayer meetings and facing frustration and guilt. Somewhere along the way, it seems we have lost our way. This book provides a positive and practical path back to the heart of what God intended prayer to be. I cannot wait for you to read it and experience the same delight I did.

Not long ago, I enjoyed the blessing of being with Daniel and his great church. The presence of the Holy Spirit was obvious among the congregation. I sensed such warmth and deep enthusiasm for the Lord. They are a praying people and have discovered the excitement of real connection with God, due largely to Pastor Henderson's leadership.

Daniel's ideas have also been a personal help to my wife, Beverly, and me. For many years, we have read the Bible and prayed together as a couple. Daniel gave me some fresh ideas about how we could use the Psalms in our devotional time. What a difference! We are grateful for Daniel's creative insights and can personally attest to their practical impact.

Beverly and I have worked for decades to bring spiritual vitality and hope to the American church and her families. This has been our passion. After all these years of intense effort and prayer, we feel that the need for a full-scale revival is greater today than ever before.

Prayer must take the central place in our churches and lives. This will require inspiring leadership and positive motivation. Daniel's years of pastoral experience and keen insights are just the kind of catalyst we need. That is why I believe God is going to use this book in a profound way to open new avenues of meaningful prayer and spark a desperately needed renewal.

If you are a pastor or church leader, please read Daniel's book carefully and put these principles into practice right away. If you know pastors who need fresh inspiration, get a copy of this book into their hands. This is the kind of book I wish I'd had many years ago as a tool to wake up our prayer meetings and inspire our people to pray with fresh vigor.

I am so glad to recommend *PRAYzing!: Creative Prayer Experiences from A to Z* to you and your entire congregation. It has been a help to my wife and me, and it will be a blessing to you. May God use it in a powerful way for His glory.

Dr. Tim LaHaye
minister, author, Christian educator

PREFACE

I rejoice to call Daniel Henderson my pastor and friend.

Daniel is rare. He is a gracious leader in love with God and God's people. I love to hear him preach and teach, and I read everything he writes, but my soul is stirred deeply when I hear him pray. The reformers of the past commonly referred to evangelical Christianity as "experiential religion." They meant that authentic Christianity is not a religion built on formulas, reason, propositional truths, codes of conduct, intellectual ascent to creedal confessions, or even scholarly exegesis, but an authentic, persistent, and glorious encounter with the living God, who reveals Himself in Christ and enlightens and empowers us through the Holy Spirit. Daniel's great delight is to guide men and women to the feet of Jesus and, because he holds tightly to the intrinsic beauty and power of the body of Christ, to do so collectively. The Scriptures come alive too.

Equally, his passion is to mentor others so that they can do the same as he. I have led prayer meetings for many, many years—some of the largest prayer meetings in history—but I welcome each opportunity to be led by and to learn from Daniel. His worship-based prayer meetings are the containment buildings for the nuclear power plant called the local church and the individual Christian life. Daniel is relentlessly calling others to join him and inviting leaders to imitate him, whether they are in front of large crowds or before an audience of One. I have accepted his invitation. I recommend you join me in celebrating *PRAYzing!*, his most recent contribution to a renewal movement desperately needed and at the center of God's heart for His people.

Under Mercy,
Dr. Bob Bakke
North American Director of the Global Day of Prayer

ACKNOWLEDGMENTS

A writing project like this is never developed in a vacuum. It is the fruit of the labors of many dear people.

First, and always, I thank my wife, Rosemary, for her partnership in life and ministry for twenty-five years. Without her loving and loyal support, I would not be in ministry today. Great is her reward in heaven.

My children—Justin, Jordan, and Heather—have kept my life fresh and fulfilling in so many ways. I am proud of the unique ways in which each of them is pursuing Christ and honoring our spiritual investment in their lives.

The living laboratory of the local church has been the "discovery zone" of virtually all my creative praying. For eleven years, the leaders and saints at Arcade Church in Sacramento, California, walked eagerly and faithfully with me in the path of innovative prayer. Since February 2004, the dear people of Grace Church have grown with me to the next level of creative experience. In so doing, they have fueled my vision. Their willingness to "do something different" has made all the difference in the world, as we have experienced the sufficiency of the Word of God, the Spirit of God, and the people of God in the context of a praying church.

The team at Strategic Renewal provides essential coordination for our growing ministry around the world. I am deeply indebted to Lori Lane Bergenstock, our ministry director, for her consistent leadership and persevering passion for our vision. The office ladies (Joyce, Mary

Ann, Sarah, Ginger, and Debby) serve with profound dedication. The board of directors provides essential guidance and accountability for all we do. Thank you, my friends. You are a treasure.

International Renewal Ministries *(PrayerSummits.Net)* first introduced me to the concept of "prayer summits" back in the early nineties. Since then, God has allowed me to implement this approach in a local church context. Today, I am honored to partner with Dennis Fuqua and his team in a variety of prayer endeavors. I thank God for their clear vision and persevering desire to call the church to Scripture-fed, Spirit-led prayer.

The team at *Pray!* Books has been a delight to work with, as always. Dave Wilson urged me to keep writing and believed in the project from the beginning. He even went to bat for my "cheesy" title. I deeply appreciate the insight and sensitivity of Susan Hay Miller in providing editorial expertise, along with so many other team members at NavPress who brought this project to fruition.

A few individuals have made unique contributions to my journey. Connie Acker provided extraordinary administrative coordination to my prayer ministry for so many years. Without her help, much of what we learned would have been squandered in the disorganization of my spontaneous approach. Alice Moss has inspired me over and over again as we have cofacilitated many prayer experiences. When it comes to prayer, we are truly "peas in a pod." Pastor Mark Vroegop graciously reviewed and improved my manuscript. He is a treasured friend, a trusted advisor, and a profoundly promising leader for a new generation of pastors.

Finally, I thank you, the reader. Your willingness to incorporate the truths and practices of this book into the fabric of your life and congregation is vital to the passion we all share for genuine revival in our land. Thank you, in advance, for taking this call seriously. I look forward to hearing your stories of PRAYzing! as we labor together for the fame of His glorious name.

Daniel Henderson

INTRODUCTION

ENCOUNTERING THE SPIRIT OF CREATIVITY

I held a familiar square of unleavened bread with the small cup of grape juice and turned to face Eugenia Mauzy. As I looked into her wise, gentle eyes, an unanticipated wave of emotion began to overwhelm my soul.

Mrs. Mauzy, a widow well into her eighties, was a humble and godly woman. Physically, Eugenia was frail. I knew it was only the Lord's strength and her sheer will to participate that allowed her to even attend this intensive three-day prayer summit. She had won my pastoral heart as she faithfully supported me on her knees during the early years of my ministry at the church.

Our group of about a hundred people sat around the rustic tables in the dining area of a Christian camp in the Sierra Nevada foothills. In a spontaneous moment of inspiration, I asked everyone to take the bread and cup and serve the person on their left. I clarified, "As you serve one another, explain what the symbols mean, how much the Lord loves the person you're serving, and why you love the person too." It seemed a good idea at the time.

It turned out to be a great idea.

Still, I could hardly contain myself as I looked into the seasoned, expectant face of this dear woman who had endured many trials in the eight decades of her life. I tried to articulate the unfathomable love and grace of Christ, then broke down as I told her how much I loved and appreciated her. We wept freely and hugged like there was no tomorrow, and we both experienced a new sense of what the Lord had in mind when He told us to remember Him. I watched with amazement as a similar sense of overwhelming commemoration became the all-encompassing experience among the entire group.

This Communion moment was just one of many Spirit-inspired "zingers" I encountered as I facilitated my first three-day prayer summit with brothers and sisters from my congregation. Throughout the event, the Lord moved my heart with creative ways to pray, worship, and respond to the Scriptures—most of which I had never even pondered and had not planned.

Even though I had previously led multiple corporate prayer times virtually every week for the past ten years, never before had I sensed this kind of direction and insight in leading other people into such meaningful, participatory experiences. Each came straight from the Bible and, I believe, straight from the heart of God through the prompting of the Holy Spirit. It was indeed the genesis of a new understanding of prayer in my pastoral ministry.

Those who know me understand that I am a "word guy." I am not much impressed with trendy church-growth movements. I study hard and try to stick close to the Book in everything I do. Of course, I have always believed and preached about the power of the Holy Spirit. Never before had I experienced the ignition of Word and Spirit in such transformational applications.

Since that summit, well over a decade ago, I have led hundreds of prayer times. Some have been small and nondescript, others very large, but each marked with a new sense of the creativity of the Holy Spirit springing from the pages of Scripture.

Over the years, hundreds of pastors have attended our church-sponsored prayer summits and "Fresh Encounter" prayer meetings. At a particular summit, pastors had traveled from faraway communities, several states, and even Canada to experience this PRAYzing! Throughout those days, I noticed the pastors taking copious notes. I assumed these were primarily journal entries about personal spiritual lessons. I discovered later that, much to my surprise, they were trying to capture and describe the particulars of these exciting moments of spontaneous prayers.

I have come to understand the extraordinary value of fresh and creative ways to use Scripture in order to engage people in meaningful, participatory prayer. I sense the time has come for me to write a book that will equip pastors, prayer leaders, and other eager Christians with the tools for experiencing a fresh creativity in prayer.

Researchers tell us that more than 90 percent of Americans pray—or at least try.[1] Most are stuck in a mode of occasional crisis-oriented requests. Many would love to learn to pray more effectively, with energy and creativity. Scripture and the Spirit can help every believer integrate innovation and practical application into every prayer experience. I earnestly hope this book will be the tool to help you do this in a new way—and for a lifetime.

Scripture and the Spirit can help every believer integrate innovation and practical application into every prayer experience.

With this earnest desire, I humbly offer *PRAYzing!* to you and your circle of fellow believers. Part 1 will give you a biblical foundation and fresh motivation for creative prayer. In part 2, I will illustrate PRAYzing! with twenty-six specific examples of how creative prayer can occur.

God longs for us to experience a fresh sense of His presence every day and every time we gather with others to seek Him. There is no limit to His creativity and no boundaries to the treasures of His Word. With the Holy Spirit's help, we can enjoy unending innovation in our prayer lives. Our hearts, our homes, our congregations, our nation, and our world will never be the same. God has entrusted that power to us through the privilege of effective prayer.

PART ONE

DISCOVERING THE POWER OF PRAYZING!

CHAPTER 1

NO MORE SLEEPY PRAYER MEETINGS

"God is not the author of boredom — especially when we are
conversing with Him."
— DANIEL HENDERSON

Let me be the first to admit that I have the problem. I have fallen asleep
in my share of prayer meetings. Sadly, I have even led some of these
supplication siestas.

My problem started as a child. It was complicated by a serious drug
issue. My parents *drug* me to church several times a week. The Wednesday
evening prayer time provided a special occasion for napping. After a few
hymns, the group commenced a long litany of boring, gossip-laden, and
seemingly tedious prayer requests. My eyes grew heavy. By the time the
people gathered in huddles, sluggishly recounting the lists of names and
problems, I had the problem. I was out like a light.

I still remember the old rousing Wednesday evening rally cry,
"Sweet Hour of Prayer." It was sweet all right. After a long day at school,
stretching my brain and wearing myself out on the playground, prayer
meeting offered a sweet and welcomed nap.

One time in college, I had a particularly embarrassing prayer nap.
I sang tenor in a traveling chorale that represented our school. We had
played at the beach all day. That night, toward the end of our church
concert, the team leader stepped to the platform to offer a closing

challenge, followed by what seemed to me to be a protracted prayer. The next thing I knew, I woke up to see the entire team (minus a tenor) standing on the platform performing the closing song. I had been out like a light, head in lap, in front of the entire church. No one on the team tried to wake me. They just enjoyed a good laugh at the expense of my drowsy nonparticipation.

SAD, SLEEPY TRADITIONS

In these and many other heavy-eyed moments of divine communion, my only comfort was in knowing that I was following the ignoble tradition of Peter, James, and John dozing on the Savior in the garden. Certainly my prayer naps were not as rude as their lethargic intercession for Jesus on His way to the cross.

Do you remember the details of this all-time low moment in the history of intercession? Jesus told His inner circle of stalwart supporters to wait in the garden while He went a little farther to pour out His soul before the Father as He paced to His agonizing death.

Within minutes, the three disciples were sawing logs. He told them, "What! Could you not watch with Me one hour? Watch and pray, lest you enter into temptation. The spirit indeed is willing, but the flesh is weak" (Matthew 26:40-41). The Greek term for "watch" literally refers to staying awake. In essence, Jesus said, "Couldn't you even stay awake with Me one hour? Wake up and pray!"

It gets worse. Two more times they dozed off on the Master. Finally, He stirred them and said, "Are you still sleeping and resting? Behold, the hour is at hand, and the Son of Man is being betrayed into the hands of sinners" (Matthew 26:45).

I cannot imagine the disappointment the Lord must have felt. As for the disciples, they were missing the real action at one of the most important moments in biblical history. I wonder how many times I have missed what God was doing because I retreated to slumberland when I should have advanced on my knees to the front lines of battle.

DECLARING WAR ON SLEEPY PRAYER MEETINGS

Over the decades, I have been in prayer meetings where participants drooled, fell over, snored, and even snorted. You have probably seen it — and done it. Somehow, I do not think God had this in mind when He commanded us to "pray in the Spirit" (Jude 20).

I have declared war on sleepy prayer meetings! As a pastor, I have been exasperated with lethargic, dozy gatherings. I do not want to attend, and I certainly do not want to lead, these dead-in-the-water prayer times.

I have discovered an approach I call worship-based prayer. These prayer times are participatory, encouraging, God-centered, and biblical. Instead of an hour of drowsy requests and pitiful pleading, fresh doses of Scripture reading and Spirit-led worship invigorate these gatherings. The foundation of these experiences is the character and Word of God, followed by spontaneous, Spirit-led surrender, intercession, and participation. My book *Fresh Encounters* tells about my journey and the dynamic ways to experience worship-based prayer.[1]

Over the years, I have learned a lot about keeping people engaged and energized in prayer. There is still much to learn, but this book will help you join me on the march against nodding off in the prayer room. This is also an important biblical command for all prayer leaders and participants.

THE BIBLICAL CALL TO PRAYZING!

When Paul wrote to the young New Testament churches, he said much about prayer. He commanded the saints to gather collectively in passionate, Spirit-guided, energized prayer. He also challenged them to stay awake!

Colossians 4:2 tells us, "Devote yourselves to prayer, keeping alert in it with an attitude of thanksgiving" (NASB). "Keeping alert" means "to stay awake." A more literal reading of Colossians 4:2 says, "Be earnest and unwearied and steadfast in your prayer [life], being [both] alert and intent in [your praying] with thanksgiving" (AMP). Eugene Peterson's rendering says, "Pray diligently. Stay alert, with your eyes wide open in gratitude" (MSG).

I'm sure Paul had heard about the heavy-eyed exploits of Peter, James, and John. He probably knew his own tendency to drift off. The Holy Spirit certainly had us in mind when He inspired this command.

In fact, this issue is so important, it is included in the great spiritual warfare passage of Ephesians 6, appearing as an exclamation point on Paul's instructions for overcoming the devil. Paul tells us that we should be "praying always with all prayer and supplication in the Spirit, *being watchful* to this end with all perseverance and supplication for all the saints" (Ephesians 6:18, emphasis added). Again, "being watchful" is a literal command to stay awake. *The Message* translates this imperative point as, "Prayer is essential in this ongoing warfare. Pray hard and long. Pray for your brothers and sisters. *Keep your eyes open.* Keep each other's spirits up so that no one falls behind or drops out" (emphasis added).

The idea is clear. Stay awake and alert! Encourage one another to wakefulness at all times and in every prayer meeting.

WHAT MUST I DO TO STAY AWAKE?

Knowing our tendency to get sleepy, remembering our Lord's disappointment with His dreamy disciples, and understanding the clear commands of the New Testament on this issue, let me ask, *Why are so many of our prayer meetings boring and lethargic? Why do we lead such drowsy prayer times?*

It may even be that sleepy, disengaged prayer meetings are sinful. Now, that thought will wake you up, won't it?

Here's the good news. Our Lord has provided everything we need to enjoy vibrant, spirited prayer meetings. His Word is a supernatural and inexhaustible guide to effective, participatory prayer. His Spirit lives within us, providing all the wisdom and creativity we need for unlimited vitality and meaningful responsiveness in our prayers. The Spirit is eagerly waiting to provide every ounce of insight we need for dynamic encounters in prayer. I like to call those moments of inspiration "PRAYzing!" — creative and transforming prayer experiences fueled by Scripture and prompted by the Holy Spirit.

A seminary degree, superior intelligence, or decades of practice are not the sources for effectiveness in prayer. Your enjoyment in prayer is not a matter of some special gift or personality style. God has provided everything for every one of us so we can pray with an alert effectiveness.

It may even be that sleepy, disengaged prayer meetings are sinful.

Yet, as a pastor, I had to learn this through experience. I have been humbled by the privilege of instructing multiplied thousands of believers in this dynamic journey of energized praying. I have even had the joy of helping countless fellow pastors with this discovery.

Most important, it will be my privilege to walk with you, in the pages of this book, with your eyes on the Scriptures and your heart yielded to the Spirit. We will discover fresh PRAYzing! for the glory of God and the good of His people.

Are you awake?

CHAPTER 2

YOUR CREATIVE HEART

"The voyage of discovery is not in seeking new landscapes
but in having new eyes."
— MARCEL PROUST

In the beginning, God created.

This first action in all of human history is also the original description of God's character.

In one moment of eternity past, nothing existed. Suddenly, by the power of the Sovereign Word, matter exploded. The eternal, self-existent almighty God spoke all that we know into reality. Everything material and spiritual began out of nothing by the imagination of the all-powerful will and Word of God.

God's name in Genesis 1:1 is "Elohim." Bible commentator Herbert Lockyer says, "Creative glory and power and God-head fullness are associated with this initial name in the Bible. . . . In *Elohim*, God is the majestic Ruler, and under such a name we have the idea of omnipotence, or creative and governing power."[1] The first sentence of the Apostles' Creed puts the creativity of God right where it belongs: "I believe in God the Father Almighty, Maker of heaven and earth."

HOW CREATIVE!

The closer you look and the broader you travel, the more you begin to fill up your cup of understanding from the ocean of God's creativity. In my limited travels, I've been awed by the grandeur of the Alps, the crystal blue waters of Cozumel, the misty mystery of Puget Sound, the plentiful fruits and flowers of Vietnam, and the spectacular brilliance of the Northern Lights. Even as a child growing up in New Mexico (not quite the "jewel" of America), the endless radiance of the White Sands National Monument, the elusive behavior of the roadrunner, the eerie magnificence of Carlsbad Caverns, and the visual splendor and aromatic stimulation of the Rocky Mountains all fascinated me.

Today, as I write this chapter, I am sitting in a beautiful lakeside home owned by some dear friends, looking over Lake Minnetonka outside Minneapolis. It is a sunny crisp day in early October. Every imaginable color captures my eye as I gaze out the large sliding glass doors. Blends of yellow, orange, red, brown, and green glimmer in the trees. The deep blue sky reflects on the rich blue-green water, rippling bright as a sparkler with the reflections of light.

Beneath the surface is a thriving collection of various fish, turtles, and swimming larvae surrounded by plant life galore. Of course, the shore of this lake is home to diverse species of wildlife including deer, turkey, squirrels, foxes, raccoons, and other assorted critters.

Flowers of purple and yellow decorate the patio outside the door as I gaze on this masterpiece. Sunshine and shadow manipulate the colors of the day. If I stepped outside for a closer look, I would soon discover a broad collection of strange insects and tiny bugs crawling on the rocks, hiding in the grass, and traversing the trees. Even now, a flock of geese is honking through the sky. All this—for the glory of the Creator.

THE CREATOR CALLS

No matter where you are, where you've been, or where you plan to go, the captivating wonder of Creator-God beckons. So now, right there where you sit, take a moment to consider His manifest beauty. Hear His call. Tune in carefully.

As you pause and drink it in, understand this certainty: Just as the eternal truth of the almighty God intersected with our world through the power of His creativity, so He invites us to cry out from this temporal realm to intersect eternity through the means of His graciously given creative power.

The work of Jesus Christ made it all possible. The Savior who created all things (see John 1:1-3; Colossians 1:16-17; Hebrews 1:2) as part of the Genesis 1 Godhead has now made us His workmanship, created in Him for good works. To guarantee that work, He has inhabited our hearts with His powerful and creative Spirit (see Romans 8:9-11).

I believe that every time we pray, God wants us to sample deeply of His inventive beauty. I often tell our congregation that worship is the response of all we are to the revelation of all He is. If this is true, how can we possibly be satisfied with bland, mindless prayers in His presence?

I also believe that every time we open the Bible in a spirit of eager communion with our loving Father, He wants to open our eyes to the vitality of His inspired truth. His Word is living and active, sharp, penetrating, revealing, and life-transforming. By the power of Scripture, He wants to create a fresher, deeper response in the soul of an ever-renewed seeker.

BE CREATIVE, LIKE YOUR GOD

Going back to Genesis, we discover God's design in creating humankind with these words: "Let Us make man in Our image, according to Our likeness" (verse 26). Theologians have grappled for years with the meaning of this declaration. What does it mean to be created in the image and likeness of God?

Among other possibilities, we must conclude that this "image" entails a profound and abounding creativity. The primary attribute of the triune God that appears prior to this point is the characteristic of God's unfathomable creativity. In Genesis 1:1-26, we find profound exhibition of the inventiveness in the divine design of our world.

> Worship is the response of all I am to the revelation of all He is.

A few verses later, God allows Adam to name all the living creatures in the garden (see Genesis 2:19). Imagine the moment. Adam can make up any syllable, vowel, guttural sound, or combination thereof that he wishes. What a blast! You can imagine him wandering through the lush, indescribably beautiful garden, just creating—coming up with ideas and names at will. God's gift of infinite creativity is unleashed as Adam walks and works in perfect communion with his Creator.

Today as we journey in the proverbial "garden of prayer," let us remember our origins. Let us consider our ancestor as he named all God's creatures with unleashed imagination, springing from intimacy with his God. Like Adam, we are made in God's image. His written Word and indwelling Spirit now instruct us. The possibilities are vast as we commune with the Father.

So, when you pray, be creative, just like God. It's who He is in you. It is what He made you to do.

CHAPTER 3

PRAYING FROM THE CREATIVE WORD

"Prayer is answering speech. The first word is God's word.
Prayer is a human word and is never the first word."
— EUGENE PETERSON

I do not always have a Bible open when I pray. As I try to awaken my heart to God during my early-morning shower, I often mumble some disjointed thoughts—but would not dare ruin my leather-bound New King James with my shampoo and shaving cream. When I receive some unexpected good news in the middle of the day, I cry out with a grateful spontaneity. There's no pressing need to go find the Good Book. When offering gratitude for a delicious meal with treasured friends around the table at a favorite restaurant, I usually do not pull out my family Bible.

When Peter was sinking in the turbulent waves of Galilee, his prayer was simple, direct, and punctuated: "Lord, save me!" (Matthew 14:30). Jesus did not rebuke him for not consulting the "text" to be sure he prayed a solid scriptural prayer. Obviously, there are times we discharge the contents of our hearts, unedited and raw. The Lord loves to hear the heart-cry of His children.

However, in the normal course of my daily time with the Lord, I always start with an open Bible. Several times a week, I lead collective prayer gatherings. Every prayer time starts with Scripture. When I facilitate three-day prayer summits, Scripture is the primary prayer tool giving fresh insight, inspiration, and articulation to our prayers. By conviction and experience, I have concluded that the most creative and effective prayers spring from the inexhaustible treasury of the Word of God. Thousands of times, I have watched the Bible expose hearts, guide language, unite diverse interests, and create indescribably powerful moments of remarkable prayer impact. Nothing is more thrilling than watching an eager group of Christians brought into unity and transformation as eyes and hearts are opened to pray from the Scriptures.

Eugene Peterson said it well:

Prayer is language used to respond to the most that has been said to us with the potential for saying all that is in us. . . . Prayer is dangerous. . . . It moves our language into potencies we are unaccustomed to and unprepared for. . . . We restore prayer to its context in God's word. Prayer is not something we think up to get God's attention or enlist his favor. Prayer is answering speech. The first word is God's word. Prayer is a human word and is never the first word, never the primary word, never the initiating and shaping word simply because we are never first; never primary. . . . The first word everywhere and always is God's word to us, not ours to him.[1]

PRAYING ON LEVEL GROUND

Peterson's insights remind me of a lesson I've learned over the years about the value of letting the Bible shape the vocabulary of prayer. It's sad, but somewhat humorous, to observe what happens in a prayer time based on stale human vocabulary rather than the fresh foundation of God's Word.

Have you been to one of those prayer times where some verbose participant blurts out a protracted prayer-speech using some cheap imitation of King James English? He even sometimes changes the tone of voice to sound more holy. It usually goes like this: "Dearest Godest, I thankest Thouest that Thouest hearest the prayers of a sainteth like me-eth. Forgiveth us of ourest iniquities and transgressions. Thou who hast madest the worldest and allest it containeth, blah, blah, blah . . ."

After ten minutes of this drivel, the dear brother finally concludes. What usually follows is unresponsive silence. The prayer meeting is dead on arrival. Most people are thinking, *Wow—how can I follow a prayer like that? I just talk like a normal person. Will God hear my simple prayer after that masterpiece?* Someone else may be wondering, *What in the world did that guy just say? How do I pray in agreement with that jumble? I didn't understand half of what he prayed.*

Finding our language in Scripture through focused and measured prayers allows everyone to discover an entry point. The Bible provides handles for mature saints and struggling neophytes. It's a wonderful thing to observe this dynamic. This is at the heart of teaching people how to truly pray.

I remember a prayer meeting in which I was instructing the group to pray from Scripture. We focused on a verse about God as our Father. I suggested that each one finish a simple sentence: "Dear God, I thank You that You are a Father who . . ." Seasoned Christians participated freely as we all responded in brief but heartfelt prayers. Then one young woman, a brand-new Christian, humbly said, "Dear God, I thank You that You are a Father who always says to me, 'I'm so glad you asked.'" How refreshing and honest! She wasn't trying to impress anyone with archaic language. On the level ground of Scripture, she was empowered to pray out in genuine, unique faith. She was simply reflecting God's heart from God's Word in God's presence. It blessed God's people.

I have often said that the best way to talk to God is in His own words. When we pray the Word of God, we embrace the will of God. The intimate and intense attention to the truth of the Word produces real worship-based prayer and all its benefits. Paul reminds us, "Let the word of Christ dwell in you richly in all wisdom, teaching and admonishing one another in psalms and hymns and spiritual songs, singing with grace in your hearts to the Lord" (Colossians 3:16).

PRAYING ON SOLID, SPIRITUAL GROUND

Of course, without the Spirit we cannot understand, apply, or pray the Word of God. In the next chapter, we will look extensively at the creative power of the Holy Spirit in our prayers. For now, let's embrace the truth that Scripture is the fuel for the Spirit's creative flames of prayer.

> *When we pray the Word of God, we embrace the will of God.*

God has allowed me to be involved in a broad circle of prayer movements, teaching around the nation in a variety of conferences and pastors' gatherings. As a result, I have encountered more than my share of unusual ideas about the role of the Holy Spirit in prayer. Sadly, many of these ideas disconnect the Spirit's work in prayer from the central place of Scripture.

An often-quoted passage is Jude 20: "But you, beloved, building yourselves up on your most holy faith, praying in the Holy Spirit." Clearly, we are to always pray in the realm of the Spirit, under His control and consistent with His character. However, I have heard all kinds of curious applications of this verse, promoting such things as bizarre emotional agitation, bodily gyrations, and even Eastern religion-style meditative mumbo jumbo. I am sure these are sincere ideas, but to disconnect this verse from the central place of the Bible is flawed exposition.

Every serious Bible student knows the importance of interpreting any individual passage in light of the context. When New Testament scholar Dr. D. A. Carson talks to pastors, he ascribes to his father, a Canadian minister, this powerful idea: "A text without a context is a pretext for a proof text." In other words, interpret a verse in light of what it was supposed to mean to people it was written to, at the time it was written in, and with the application it was meant to have.

So, what is the correlation between our "most holy faith" and praying in the Spirit? Throughout his small epistle, Jude writes primarily to counter false teachers, apostasy, and the fruit of ungodly living. In verse three he writes, "I found it necessary to write to you exhorting you to contend earnestly for the faith which was once for all delivered to the saints." This "faith" is the completed Word of God and His gospel given to the church. The "most holy faith" by which we are to pray in the Holy Spirit is a focus on being rooted in solid content, not launched into some paranormal behavior.

Ephesians 6:17-18 also connects the Spirit and the Word in prayer: "And take the helmet of salvation, and the sword of the Spirit, which is the word of God; praying always with all prayer and supplication in the Spirit." Praying "in the Spirit" again appears in direct connection to our sure salvation and the spoken Word of God.

I know this is starting to sound like a theology lesson. Still, it is vital to understand that our creativity in prayer must be consistent with the Word and will of the Creator. The Bible must remain central if we are to get creative without getting crazy.

PRAYING FROM MEANINGFUL GROUND

As I complete this chapter, our church is at the end of a focus we call "Seek Week." Among other emphases, we've been gathering in the early morning with a goal of seeking the Lord. Each morning, I have used a passage of Scripture to guide our prayers of surrender and spiritual resolve.

Today around lunchtime, one of our staff members pulled me aside to thank me for the power of this emphasis. She said,

> I never realized how simple but meaningful this kind of prayer can be. I've been in attendance each morning and tried to sit in several parts of the room so that I can pray with different

people. Yesterday, I was in a small group with four others. Each responded so sincerely as they prayed Scripture. It moved me to the point that I wanted to place my hand on each one just to let them know I understood and agreed with them in prayer. It was so very moving. The Spirit was really at work, and I love learning how to pray straight from the Bible.

Jonathan Edwards, a pastor and theologian who lived in the 1700s, emphasized the power and centrality of the Scriptures for effective prayer when he wrote:

The Spirit who causes men to have greater regard for the Holy Scriptures and establishes them more in their truth and divine inspiration is certainly the Spirit of God. . . . It is this very word that God has given to be the great and standing rule for the direction of His church in all spiritual matters and for all concerns of their souls in all ages. A spirit of delusion will not incline persons to seek direction from the mouth of God.[2]

"Seek direction from the mouth of God." What a concept! This is the key idea and the central passion of the artistic pray-er. It is the centerpiece of an innovative prayer gathering. Real, ingenious prayer cherishes direction from the mouth and heart of the Creator.

Only here do we discover the kind of prayers that capture the imagination, move the heart, and transform the church on its knees.

CHAPTER 4

PRAYING WITH CREATIVE CONFIDENCE

"An essential aspect of creativity is not being afraid to fail."
— DR. EDWIN LAND

"The intuitive mind is a sacred gift and the rational mind is a faithful servant. We have created a society that honors the servant and has forgotten the gift."
— ALBERT EINSTEIN

I still remember the first time I jumped off a cliff. Thirty-five feet spanned the distance between my perilous perch and the inviting blue water of Lake Tahoe. It felt like a hundred.

My potential watery plunge was uncharted territory. I did not know if the smack of hitting the surface would hurt. I was not completely sure of the depth of the water. I hoped I could jump out far enough to miss the protrusions in the cliff below.

Witnessing two friends leaping and loving it finally encouraged some trusting assumptions in my mind. Eventually pride and curiosity for the adventure overcame me. Geronimo! What a rush. Soon, the fright of my first launch evaporated into the exhilaration of the repeated adrenaline blast. I think I made the jump about five times that day.

Uncharted territory. For some, the very idea evokes fearful emotions and a tendency to recoil, like standing on the perch of that cliff. For others, the "unknown" motivates an ever-ready spirit of adventure. When it comes to leading a prayer time, the idea of uncharted territory can strike terror in the soul.

As I have had the occasion to train hundreds of church leaders and prayer facilitators in the dynamics of leading effective prayer times, I have been surprised at how many are cautious and reluctant to step out in providing creative guidance. They do not want to do anything too bizarre. No one wants to mislead the saints, especially in prayer. Others just do not know how to distinguish between the prompting of the Holy Spirit, the emotion of the moment, and a bad case of heartburn.

Granted, it has been a long time since anyone has seen handwriting on a wall. Don't count on a mighty rushing wind to blow every time you try to find a fresh direction in the prayer meeting. A voice from the rafters might not be the Lord but a construction worker trying to fix the heating vents.

Prayer is the call to experience things previously unknown to us, but familiar to God.

In a sense, every prayer occasion is a jump into uncharted territory, whether private or in a group. Prayer is the call to experience things previously unknown to us, but familiar to God. The invitation appears full of risk and bursting with the possibility of stumbling. Some never really take the leap in their own hearts; most never do so in community. The ones I have watched do it are forever changed and empowered.

DECIDING TO JUMP IN

It is a great loss to miss the exhilarating thrill of creative prayer. Brennan Manning says,

> Each of us pays a price for our fear of falling flat on our face. It assures the progressive narrowing of our personalities and

prevents exploration and experimentation. As we get older, we do only those things we do well. There is no growth in the Christ Jesus without some difficulty and fumbling. If we are going to keep on growing, we must keep on risking failure throughout our lives.[1]

The potential of failure and fumbling paralyzes us as we consider the risks of leading prayer. Many get stuck in feelings of inadequacy. Others allow a fear of man to overshadow their determination to pursue the face of God. From God's vantage point, prayer is packed with unexpected grace and elating spiritual experience. He invites us to insightful, continuous growth on the creative prayer path.

A TRUSTED GUIDE INTO THE UNKNOWN

One secret to taking on any uncharted territory is the assistance of an experienced mentor. Serious hunters hire guides who can lead them to the big herd of trophy elk. Earnest health nuts secure the services of trainers who understand how to get results in conditioning and weight loss.

We have the consummate guide for every expedition in prayer through the Spirit of the indwelling Christ. He sees and knows it all as familiar and spectacular terrain. He has been there before. He is there already, inviting us to join Him.

LAUNCHING INTO THE DEPTHS

For many years, I have felt a special fascination with the statement Jesus made to Peter in Luke 5:4, "Launch out into the deep and let down your nets for a catch." We all sense regular challenges from the Lord to take a step of faith into the deeper waters. It's a journey of learning to trust His direction and observe the extraordinary results. This is always true in the arena of leading in prayer. Jesus still calls us outside the comfort zone of our logic and experience.

In Luke's account, we know Jesus was setting up Peter and his associates for a lesson on faith. He wanted them to clearly understand the power and sufficiency of His way and will for their lives. Peter reacted to Jesus' command from his own natural judgment: "Master, we have toiled all night and caught nothing; nevertheless at Your word I will let down the net" (Luke 5:5). Peter seemed a bit hesitant in his obedience as he picked up his nets and thrust his little boat into the deeper water.

As the story unfolds, they catch a "great number of fish" (Luke 5:6). The nets were so overloaded they were breaking. Peter and Andrew called their fishing partners over to help, and the fishermen packed both boats beyond capacity.

What else could Peter do but fall at Jesus' feet and declare, "Depart from me, for I am a sinful man, O Lord!" (Luke 5:8). The regret of not trusting the Master's direction was coupled with a deep astonishment over what had just happened.

The whole group was learning a lesson in belief. This profound fishing story was just a warm-up for greater things. The Lord made this clear when He told Peter, "Do not be afraid. From now on you will catch men." Their response this time? "So when they had brought their boats to land, they forsook all and followed Him" (Luke 5:11).

I think they got it.

ACCEPTING THE CHALLENGE

I believe the Lord Jesus challenges us on a regular basis to "launch out into the deep" and cast our nets into the depths of His sufficiency to harvest unexpected and astonishing experiences of His presence and power. We must ask what keeps us from authentic trust in His promptings. What harvest of blessing might unfold before our eyes if we would just take the step of obedience?

Like Peter, we doubt. We rest on the status quo of past experiences.

We fail to lean on the competency of God's character and direction. We cannot see the richness of all He has prepared for us just beneath the surface of our limited understanding. He knows the possibilities are truly mind-boggling. We must choose to walk by faith, not just predictable and safe "seeing."

I have learned the lesson repeatedly. God is Lord of the prayer time. He wants it to be an encounter of rich meaning and compelling participation. He calls me to let my net down into the treasure of His Word, trusting the genius of His Spirit and enjoying the abundance of His provision and presence.

POWER FOR THE INCAPABLE

How can common individuals really lead others into uncommon and powerfully creative prayer experiences? The actual answer is: They can't. Yet the ultimate answer is that the Spirit of Christ, living and working in them, can lead through them to make every prayer gathering a meaningful and transforming experience.

Just as Christ was all-wise and all-sufficient that day with Peter on the Galilean lake, He is fully capable in and through you as you journey into the uncharted territory of greater depths in prayer. He reveals His wisdom and direction by the power of His very life living in you by the Holy Spirit.

The Holy Spirit is not some ethereal concept or distant power. He is not some laughing gas or glow-in-the-dark liquid. He is the very presence of the almighty Creator, living in our hearts to accomplish God's will, for Christ's honor. It is God's desire that His people pray effectively, powerfully, and creatively. It is for God's glory when they do. And they will—when they know the character and work of the Holy Spirit. Let's get reintroduced so we can make a courageous leap, repeatedly, into uncharted territory.

FIRST STEPS FOR TAKING THE PLUNGE INTO PRAYZING:

- Find where people are praying biblically and creatively—and go there! (You can find helpful resources and learn of some compelling prayer opportunities at www.strategicrenewal.com.)
- Listen, learn, and participate.
- Start transforming your areas of ministry and life into prayer-oriented experiences. Let prayer become a natural part of the character of your life and the culture of your ministry.
- Don't wait until you are ready. Just do it! Trusting the Word and Spirit only happens when you are actually praying (not just thinking, talking, or reading about praying).

CHAPTER 5

TRUSTING HIS CREATIVE INSTINCTS

"A hunch is creativity trying to tell you something."
— FRANK CAPRA

"O God the Holy Spirit,
Thou who dost proceed from the Father and the Son,
Have mercy on me,
When thou didst first hover over chaos, order came to birth,
Beauty robed the world, fruitfulness sprang forth.
Move, I pray thee, upon my disordered heart."
— A PURITAN PRAYER

At our three-day prayer summits, we are intentional to throw willing hearts into the "deep end" of creative prayer leadership. Prior to every summit, we select fifteen to twenty facilitators. After some orientation, we assign each one to serve as part of a leadership team. They assist me in offering direction for our large-group prayer sessions and working with two or three others in leading the small-group prayer sessions. Keep in mind, these worship-based segments of prayer often last two to three hours each. The time spent is necessary for providing creative, insightful leadership.

Several times a day during the summit, we meet as facilitators to discuss the progress of the gathering and the dynamics of what is occurring in the groups. This allows me to give pastoral oversight to the effectiveness of each facilitator, provide training, and get a better sense of the overall themes and focal points emerging in lives and hearts.

One of the great thrills of my life is hearing the reports of how each person has sensed the practical leadership of the Holy Spirit in the prayer times. With unbridled enthusiasm, facilitators will often turn to a passage of Scripture and explain how the Lord gave them insight in how the group could pray. Some report powerful spiritual breakthroughs when people were encouraged to respond to the Word and Spirit in a specific focus of prayer.

> *To know the Holy Spirit is to trust the Holy Spirit. To trust the Holy Spirit is to act and react in full confidence of His creative power in your life.*

I have come to believe that God's norm is creative, compelling prayer experiences and that every Spirit-indwelt believer can discover this reality on a regular basis. To know the Holy Spirit is to trust the Holy Spirit. To trust the Holy Spirit is to act and react in full confidence of His creative power in your life. I believe every Christian can experience this practical leadership of the Holy Spirit in order to trust His direction and follow His promptings? How can we do this in a fashion that is biblical, edifying to participants, and honoring to His name? This chapter is the need-to-know summary for real PRAYzing!

THE CREATOR WITHIN

In Genesis 1:2, the triune God looked over a formless, empty mass. The Spirit of God "hovered" over the amorphous abyss of raging, chaotic waters. Suddenly, at the will and voice of God, light appeared. Soon, all that we know existed in fullness, order, and beauty.

That Spirit lives in your heart. I love the word picture of the Spirit "hovering" over the waters. The Hebrew word for *hovering* means "to move gently, to softly brood" or even "to fertilize." Like those primordial waters, our prayer times are often empty and formless—even chaotic! Yet the Spirit works gently to fertilize our hearts with His word and enliven our minds to discover His will in these important experiences.

BLESSED ASSURANCE

Imagine the emotions of the disciples in the Upper Room hours before the betrayal and trial of Jesus as it was becoming progressively and painfully clear that He was about to depart this world. He knew their anxiety and turmoil, often referring to their need for peace in those moments of final instruction (see John 14:1,27; 16:6,20,22,33).

Jesus was leaving them, but He was not abandoning them. They had experienced the beauty of His personal presence for about three years. As He talked about His departure, He promised them His continued personal presence.

In summary, Jesus assured the disciples of His extravagant provision of peace and power through His Spirit living in them. His assurances were clear and compelling and constituted a call to profound exploits for His ongoing glory. Hang with me as we make a quick survey. Hear the call again in order to live and pray by the power of this promised Spirit.

> "And I will pray the Father, and He will give you another Helper, that He may abide with you forever—the Spirit of truth, whom the world cannot receive, because it neither sees Him nor knows Him; but you know Him, for He dwells with you and will be in you. I will not leave you orphans; I will come to you." (John 14:16-18)

In knowing Christ, we have the confidence that the Spirit is abiding in us and is the personal presence of God in our hearts, communicating the *truth* of the word of God. Christ declared that we would *know* the

Holy Spirit. We will live and lead in the confident knowledge of the Holy Spirit, as promised by Jesus, trusting the truth of His character in us.

"These things I have spoken to you while being present with you. But the Helper, the Holy Spirit, whom the Father will send in My name, He will teach you all things, and bring to your remembrance all things that I said to you." (John 14:25-26)

The Holy Spirit *is* helping us, teaching us, and prompting us to think about the truths of Christ. We will trust in His peace and not doubt or be anxious. He will bring to mind the various ways that the Word of God applies to life. He continually teaches us how to follow Christ, as revealed through the written Word of God.

"But when the Helper comes, whom I shall send to you from the Father, the Spirit of truth who proceeds from the Father, He will testify of Me. And you also will bear witness, because you have been with Me from the beginning." (John 15:26-27)

The Spirit will help us know Christ and point others to Him as we lead in His power. Right now, the Spirit proceeds as a gift from the Father to our hearts and through our lives to honor Christ and fulfill His will.

"Nevertheless I tell you the truth. It is to your advantage that I go away; for if I do not go away, the Helper will not come to you; but if I depart, I will send Him to you. And when He has come, He will convict the world of sin, and of righteousness, and of judgment: of sin, because they do not believe in Me; of righteousness, because I go to My Father and you see Me no more; of judgment, because the ruler of this world is judged.

"I still have many things to say to you, but you cannot bear them now. However, when He, the Spirit of truth, has come, He will guide you into all truth; for He will not speak on His own authority, but whatever He hears He will speak; and He will tell you things to come. He will glorify Me, for He will take of what is Mine and declare it to you. All things that the Father has are Mine. Therefore I said that He will take of Mine and declare it to you." (John 16:7-15)

We can trust the Holy Spirit to work in our hearts to expose our sin, lead us in righteousness, and judge our thoughts and intentions. We can live and pray in the absolute *promise* that the Spirit will guide us into a clear understanding of biblical truth. We can trust that the Spirit will provide all the fullness of the Father and Son in our minds and hearts to lead in a way that glorifies Christ.

Jesus provided profound insight and inspired real confidence in the hearts of His disciples. Receive those words and walk in them as you pray.

LIVING IT OUT IN NEW TESTAMENT MINISTRY

I also love the way other New Testament Scripture explodes our preconceived limitations and elucidates the possibilities of the Spirit's leadership in our lives. Proceed and read with care.

Paul's inspired instruction in Romans 8:16 tells us, "The Spirit Himself bears witness with our spirit that we are children of God." What does it mean for the Spirit to "bear witness" with ours? Another version says, "His Holy Spirit speaks to us deep in our hearts" (NLT). The Spirit communicates to us in our hearts, assuring us of His presence and our sonship. The Greek verb "bears witness" is in the present tense and active voice. This means that right now, and constantly, the Spirit is initiating and confirming in a straightforward manner with our hearts. He is speaking truth to my spirit and yours, if you know Christ.

The message of Romans 8:16 is an encouraging confirmation, reminding us of our standing as children and all the treasures that belong to us through our inheritance. While this may be the most significant message the Spirit communicates to us in our Christian journey, obviously it is not the only message He speaks.

The Spirit of God is not inactive or mute. He is not in retirement at a beach home in Florida. He is not distracted with other things. His primary purpose and ministry is in us, among us, and through us for the glory of Christ and the advancement of the gospel. We can trust Him.

> *The Spirit of God is not inactive or mute. He is not in retirement at a beach home in Florida. He is not distracted with other things.*

Here we find all the assurance we need to experience real PRAYzing! Jesus promises that the Spirit of God, living and active in our hearts, will lead us to understand the content and application of all truth. He will guide us consistently with His revealed Word. This will and should occur in the most practical ways. It will happen for the glory of God and will always be evidence of the work and heart of Christ.

CONFIDENT CREATIVITY!

The Bible urges us to experience the real and practical leadership of the Holy Spirit in our lives: "For as many as are led by the Spirit of God, these are sons of God" (Romans 8:14). This is the essence of praying in the Spirit, as commanded in Ephesians 6:18 and Jude 20. God is working in us "to will and to do for His good pleasure" (Philippians 2:13).

The *modus operandi* for a true disciple is the clear leadership of the Holy Spirit. Nehemiah 9:20 declares, "You also gave Your good Spirit to instruct them." We can pray confidently, "Teach me to do Your will, for

You are my God; Your Spirit is good. Lead me in the land of upright-ness" (Psalm 143:10).

Now step outside the box of all the lazy, dozy, cozy prayer times you have experienced in the past and try this perspective on for size:

But as it is written:

"Eye has not seen, nor ear heard,
nor have entered into the heart of man
the things which God has prepared for those who love Him."

But God has revealed them to us through His Spirit. For the Spirit searches all things, yes, the deep things of God. For what man knows the things of a man except the spirit of the man which is in him? Even so no one knows the things of God except the Spirit of God. Now we have received, not the spirit of the world, but the Spirit who is from God, that we might know the things that have been freely given to us by God.

These things we also speak, not in words which man's wisdom teaches but which the Holy Spirit teaches, comparing spiritual things with spiritual. But the natural man does not receive the things of the Spirit of God, for they are foolish-ness to him; nor can he know them, because they are spiritu-ally discerned. But he who is spiritual judges all things, yet he himself is rightly judged by no one. For "who has known the mind of the LORD that he may instruct Him?" But we have the mind of Christ. (1 Corinthians 2:9-16)

Here we find the long-term confidence and expectation for unlim-ited PRAYzing! There is no boundary to what the Spirit wants to reveal to us about the depth and sufficiency of His Word. The Spirit in us knows the deep things of God and wants to reveal them to us. This will not occur in some superficial capacity of mere words. The Spirit will allow us to compare spiritual things with spiritual things, leading to profound insight. All of this is to be consistent with the mind of Christ.

THE SPIRIT'S LEADING ROLE

The classic passage on prayer found in Romans 8:26-27 tells us,

> Likewise the Spirit also helps in our weaknesses. For we do not know what we should pray for as we ought, but the Spirit Himself makes intercession for us with groanings which cannot be uttered. Now He who searches the hearts knows what the mind of the Spirit is, because He makes intercession for the saints according to the will of God.

We would be at a complete loss of clarity and communication except that the Spirit works on our behalf to sort out the deep feelings and emotions of the heart, shaping them in compliance to the will of God.

Without taking time for extensive analysis and exposition, it is obvious that insightful prayer is only possible by the tutelage of the Holy Spirit. Prayer calls us into a mystery beyond our limited human comprehension. We would be at a complete loss of clarity and communication except that the Spirit works on our behalf to sort out the deep feelings and emotions of the heart, shaping them in compliance to the will of God.

Ephesians 5:18-21 gives us the confidence in knowing that when we are "filled with the Spirit" (controlled by His influence), we will effectively engage with others in "psalms and hymns and spiritual songs, singing and making melody" in our hearts to the Lord.

This underscores the leading role of the Holy Spirit and specifies the result of His influence in our midst.

So, living in the reality and realm of the Spirit, we are now to "walk in the Spirit" (Galatians 5:25). This clearly includes our walk of prayer. Therefore, next time you stroll to your favorite chair to commune with God or enter a room of eager prayer warriors, walk with expectation and confidence. Walk in the Holy Spirit.

THE PRAYER LEADER'S CHECKLIST FOR TRUSTING THE LEADERSHIP OF THE HOLY SPIRIT

When you feel prompted to pray in a certain direction or focus on specific issues, ask these questions to determine if you're on the right track:

- Am I fully surrendered to the Holy Spirit?
- Is this direction based in Scripture?
- Will this prompting glorify Jesus?
- Is this prayer for now or later?
- Is this prayer just for me or for the whole group?
- Does this focus lead to worship and mutual edification?
- Will this direction promote the fruit (character) of the Holy Spirit?
- Will this focus unite our hearts (rather than confuse or distract)?
- Can this focus facilitate the convicting work of the Holy Spirit in some way?

- Will it help give language to prayer according to the will of God?
- Will this direction enhance our united participation in worship through psalms, hymns, and spiritual songs?

CHAPTER 6

CLUES FOR CREATIVITY

"Prayers which are in accordance with God's will originate from God, are revealed to us by the Holy Spirit, and return to God through prayers. Whatever prayer is in accordance with God's will must begin with God's will; men merely respond to, and transmit, this will."
— WATCHMAN NEE

"When it comes to prayer, we must remember that God is not the author of confusion, nor is He the author of conformity. He is, however, the author of creativity."
— DANIEL HENDERSON

In my previous book, *Fresh Encounters*, I wrote extensively about a balanced, biblical pattern for prayer, based on the model Jesus gave to His disciples in Matthew 6:9-13 (the Lord's Prayer). An understanding of this pattern provides a valuable grid for facilitating creative prayer.

This is patterned after the 4/4 musical beat of a conductor. As a prayer tool, it is an effective way by which the Holy Spirit can direct our hearts with fresh creativity in our prayer times.

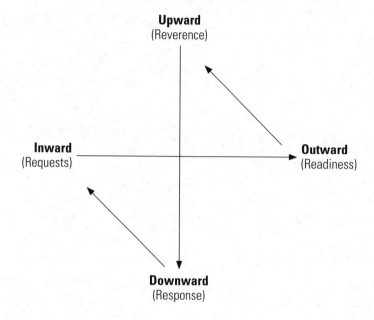

Upward
(Reverence)

Inward
(Requests)

Outward
(Readiness)

Downward
(Response)

THE STARTING PLACE: REVERENCE

The conductor raises a hand and fixes it at a point in the air to capture the attention of the musicians. Everyone gets ready to begin. In the prayer pattern Jesus gave His disciples, He instructs us to begin with a focus of worship ("Our Father in Heaven, hallowed be Your name . . ."). We call this upward focus the "Reverence" stroke. This is the concept I call worship-based, rather than need-based, prayer. It begins with the character of God as we take time to focus our entire beings on the wonders of who God is.

THE DOWNWARD STROKE: RESPONSE

The conductor gives the downbeat, and the music begins. Jesus taught a second element of biblical prayer when He said, "Your kingdom come. Your will be done on earth as it is in heaven." This stroke is our response to God's character in prayer. This involves yielding to the control of the Holy Spirit and recommitting to God's kingdom purposes. Introspection and surrender mark this time of response. It is a season of pledged obedience to the will and Word of God, desiring the accomplishment of His will in our lives.

THE INWARD STROKE: REQUESTS

From the downbeat, the conductor now moves the baton to the left, setting the tempo for the music.

"Give us this day our daily bread and forgive us our trespasses as we forgive those who trespass against us." This is the next element Christ teaches in His model prayer. This involves a period of heartfelt requests with the themes of provision and purity.

Of course, Jesus has just said that our Father knows our needs before we ask (see Matthew 6:8). This is not a time of informing God of our needs as much as it is a conscious trust in God as the perfect definer and provider of our needs. It involves prayer about personal requests and the concerns of others. This focus also includes corporate concerns, such as congregational challenges or broader issues in the body of Christ. In all this, recognize that "God shall supply all your needs according to His riches in glory in Christ Jesus" (Philippians 4:19, NASB).

Not only is God's provision a key concern during this stroke, but so is purity. As we willingly enter the forgiveness process—in both directions—we commit ourselves to lives of purity, living with a clear conscience before God and others. We pledge to seek and extend forgiveness daily. Purity is the key to harmony and unity in the body of Christ and must not be neglected in our daily time with the Lord.

THE OUTWARD STROKE: READINESS

The conductor moves the beat to the right, keeping tempo. The outward stroke reminds us of the spiritual contest before us and, more important, reassures us of the spiritual resources within us.

When we pray, "Lead us not into temptation but deliver us from evil," we recognize our own inability to overcome the temptations and attacks of daily life. We entrust our welfare for the warfare to the delivering force of our Divine Enabler, often through the power of His promises.

THE UPWARD STROKE: REVERENCE

With an upward motion, the conductor returns the beat to the starting point. The traditional version we recite of this model prayer concludes on a high note of praise: "For Yours is the Kingdom, and the Power, and the Glory forever. Amen." Again, you can enjoy a more thorough development of these points in *Fresh Encounters*.

KEYS TO CREATIVE INSIGHT

For our purposes, let us take this pattern one more step to clarify practical handles for praying more innovatively. I call these the *who, how, what*, and *where* of creative prayer.

Here are the basic questions that stimulate Spirit-given insight that can be useful to prompt responsive prayer:

- *Who* is God?
- *How* should we respond?
- *What* should we do about it?
- *Where* do we go from here?

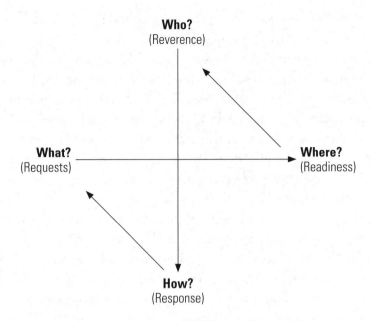

Who?
(Reverence)

What?
(Requests)

Where?
(Readiness)

How?
(Response)

As you look at any passage, first ask, "Who is God?" Invite the Holy Spirit to give you understanding of what the text tells you about the character of God. Assuming you are in a group prayer time, ask others to contribute their insights from the text. It is truly astonishing to discover so many truths about God's nature, names, and person in the texts of the Bible.

Second, notice insights about "How should we respond?" Again, the passage will often give direct clues of expressions of surrender to the will and kingdom of God. Look for such terminology as "I will" or "I have." Take note of positive action verbs such as "trust," "praise," "worship," or "cry out." Observe willful declarations such as "I will not be afraid," "I will walk," or "I will not turn away."

Third, consider the question, "What should we pray about?" Often a passage will contain specific requests or express certain desires that can form a basis of our own prayers. Look for fears, struggles, needs, decisions, challenges, and longings. Again, these observations foster creative ways to invite participants to pray in similar practical fashion.

The fourth area of discovery involves the question, "Where do we go from here?" Most texts will speak of some challenge or spiritual enemy to overcome. Often these ideas will guide the participants in identifying and anticipating practical spiritual battles. With the Spirit's insight, you can use these themes to guide others into meaningful prayer.

Consistent with the pattern of the traditional Lord's Prayer, seasons of prayer should end with praise and declarations of God's power and rule. Often a closing song can accomplish this purpose.

This biblical pattern can assist you in most prayer experiences. Look for creative entry points at any of these four expressions. If you want, use the suggested arrow system to mark potential PRAYzing! In the appendix of this book, you will find an example of how this can work in a word-focused, worship-based prayer time.

The Holy Spirit is the vital source for all we need. These concepts will serve as simple tools. Ultimately, insight from the Word and illumination by the Spirit will be sufficient in any occasion to provide the inspiration you need for the innovation you seek. Insight plus illumination results in inspiration and innovation.

All of this is a gift from God, for His people and ultimately for His glory. I have seen it happen hundreds of times. Join me now as we share twenty-six glimpses of the practicality of how this all works.

PART TWO

HOW PRAYZING! HAPPENS

So far, we have learned and affirmed that God is not the author of sleepy, dull prayer times. His Word is an unlimited treasure chest filled with truth that fuels meaningful prayer. His creative presence abides in us through the Holy Spirit. His Spirit is fully alive and eagerly waiting to provide every ounce of insight and direction needed for dynamic encounters in prayer.

"Zing" is a lively aspect of an experience that makes the occasion particularly enjoyable, even giving us a surge of strength. Other words that convey "zing" might be energy, fervor, passion, vigor, zeal, and zest. At the other end of the spectrum are lethargy and sluggishness.

The following A-to-Z guide illustrates PRAYzing! as I have experienced it over the years in a variety of settings. These examples are not designed for some mechanical duplication in your next prayer time. To pray by "imitation" rather than by "inspiration" contradicts all that we have taught so far. The goal is not to try to mimic these experiences; rather, let them serve to help you think beyond the box of predictability the next time you pray—and the time after that, and the time after that. You will see how Scripture can come to life, with the innovative insight of the Holy Spirit, to provide compelling and participatory moments of dynamic prayer.

Throughout this book, I refer to certain kinds of prayer times. In my pastoral ministry, I have identified some experiences with certain labels. The following gives a description of each to help you understand the context and content of these experiences:

Powerhouse Prayer—Worship-based prayer meetings held on Sunday mornings designed to provide intercessory prayer support for the church services.

Fresh Encounter—A regular (weekly or monthly) church-wide, worship-based prayer gathering designed to involve the entire congregation in meaningful worship, shared prayer support, and strategic intercessory focus on the overall ministry and direction of the church.

Prayer Summits—Two- or three-day unscripted prayer retreats designed to facilitate free-flowing Scripture reading, singing, responsive prayer, and mutual confession and intercession. Typically, we have held annual women's, men's, and all-church prayer summits.

Staff Prayer Time—Regular times of prayer with church staff.

Seek Week—Scheduled for the first week of the year in place of normal ministry activities, featuring extraordinary times of corporate prayer.

Forty-Day Spiritual Discovery—A church-wide season of study, prayer, and fasting designed for personal and corporate spiritual renewal. Pastors write the forty-day study guide specifically for the congregation.

AWESOME WONDER

By the word of the LORD the heavens were made,
And all the host of them by the breath of His mouth.
He gathers the waters of the sea together as a heap;
He lays up the deep in storehouses.
Let all the earth fear the LORD;
Let all the inhabitants of the world stand in awe of Him.
For He spoke, and it was done;
He commanded, and it stood fast.
(PSALM 33:6-9)

One hundred twenty-five men gathered on a Thursday evening at a retreat center in northern Minnesota. The prayer summit idea was new to the congregation at this point, so many were a bit cautious about this rather radical prayer event. We had no agenda, a loose schedule, plenty of freedom, and three days before us. It all felt strange to some.

After walking through the normal orientation we use to help establish the guidelines for our days of prayer, we commenced. Men were encouraged to start a song, read Scripture, lead in a responsive reading from the Bible, and participate as the Spirit directed. Soon they seemed to be getting the idea, and things were flowing along.

After "camping out" around several themes, we arrived at a focus on the awesomeness of God. We read many verses and, not surprisingly, sang, "Awesome God" and "I Stand in Awe of You." On the heels of that song, I referenced Psalm 33:8, "Let all the inhabitants of the world stand in awe of Him." I asked the men to tell the Lord why they stood in awe of Him. I queried, "What is it about God that causes you to feel awe and wonder in His presence? Just pray out, 'I stand in awe of you, O God, because . . .'"

As an aside, you will find that I often use simple prayer entry points when praying in a large group. This allows even the most reserved and cautious participants to feel they can join in. It also keeps the more verbose folks from hijacking the prayer time with some extended treatise. Further, it encourages meaningful specificity in the prayers. One other benefit is that it allows individuals to pray many times, yet with a different application and in succinct fashion.

In this case, it worked well. While some men were cautious, they felt they could participate in a brave way. One after another, men opened their hearts to the almighty God and one another in giving specific reasons for their awe and praise of God.

We began to echo, as we often do, an affirming united word after each prayer. We all cried out, "Let all the earth fear the Lord." This went on for a while with moments of great crescendo punctuated by seasons of quiet reflection.

As the evening was ending, I took the men outside their comfort zone in another step of creative prayer. Noting the clear night sky and the unseasonable, pleasant fall weather, I asked the men to join me outside for a final moment of praise. As we walked out the doors into a clearing next to the building, we repeatedly sang "Awesome God."

Once all the men were outside, I asked each to look to the sky and stand in absolute silence as we considered the truths of God's Word in

Psalm 33:6, "By the word of the LORD the heavens were made, and all the host of them by the breath of His mouth."

After about five minutes of silence, gazing on this breathtaking celestial wonder, we sang all four verses of "How Great Thou Art." The experience was truly spine-tingling as the voices of 125 men echoed across the field under the magnificent night sky.

Just as we ended, a man visiting from another church broke out a super-powered laser pointer. He knew his stuff. He began to point out various planets and constellations with a beam that seemed to penetrate the heavens. As a student of astronomy, he identified the Milky Way and many obscure points of interest as we listened in captivation. After he was finished, we sang another chorus of "How Great Thou Art" with minds that were even more boggled by the majesty and awesomeness of our God.

B

BEAUTIFUL TO ME BECAUSE . . .

One thing I have desired of the LORD,
That will I seek:
That I may dwell in the house of the LORD
All the days of my life,
To behold the beauty of the LORD,
And to inquire in His temple.
(PSALM 27:4)

And let the beauty of the LORD our God be upon us,
And establish the work of our hands for us;
Yes, establish the work of our hands.
(PSALM 90:17)

Honor and majesty are before Him;
Strength and beauty are in His sanctuary.
(PSALM 96:6)

At a prayer summit many years ago, the large group landed on the theme of the beauty of God. By the prompting of the Holy Spirit, we were able to turn a very good spiritual focus into a powerfully specific expression of the splendor and majesty of God.

Let me illustrate. My wife, Rosemary, is beautiful. Most people these days think she is my daughter when they see us together. I am bald, prematurely wrinkled, and just an average Joe. Somehow, the Lord temporarily blinded her during our days of dating and engagement. After the wedding, it was too late! She was stuck with my common appearance.

Now, I could simply say, "Rosemary, you are beautiful." Depending on the passion and sincerity of the statement, it may thrill her heart. However, if I get specific, she will love hearing my description of her attractiveness even more.

I could praise her for her smooth, youthful skin. I could tell her how much I love her picture-perfect teeth and engaging smile. I could speak romantically of her alluring hazel-colored eyes or her beautiful brunette hair. (I had better stop—I am starting to breathe heavily even as I write.) Nevertheless, you get the idea.

When it comes to the Lord, it is good for us, and glorious to Him, to be specific about His beauty. So in this moment of prayer, I instructed this circle of about 150 men and women to consider how they might extol the Lord with this sentence: "Lord, You are beautiful to me because . . ."

To give them a moment to consider how the Spirit might be directing their response, we repeated the simple chorus, "O Lord, You're Beautiful." As the singing commenced, the declarations arose. This chorus of declaring the beauty of our God in very specific and personal ways was striking. Some examples were:

Lord, You are beautiful to me because . . .

. . . You love me just as I am.

. . . You never change.

. . . You created all that is beautiful.

. . . You are the object of worship of myriads of angels.

. . . You have made my life beautiful.

. . . You have created new beauty in my marriage.

You can imagine the exhilaration of this kind of praise continuing for at least twenty minutes, as it did. It was truly beautiful in the ultimate sense. It has been said that nothing is dynamic until it is specific. Dynamic beauty. The beauty of God. How glorious is that?

CRYING OUT

As Jesus continued on toward Jerusalem, he reached the border between Galilee and Samaria. As he entered a village there, ten lepers stood at a distance, crying out, "Jesus, Master, have mercy on us!" He looked at them and said, "Go show yourselves to the priests." And as they went, their leprosy disappeared. One of them, when he saw that he was healed, came back to Jesus, shouting, "Praise God, I'm healed!" He fell face down on the ground at Jesus' feet, thanking him for what he had done. This man was a Samaritan. Jesus asked, "Didn't I heal ten men? Where are the other nine? Does only this foreigner return to give glory to God?" And Jesus said to the man, "Stand up and go. Your faith has made you well."
(LUKE 17:11-19, NLT)

The church leadership team sat in a circle at a nearby retreat center. This was our first "Leadership Prayer Summit." About two dozen pastors and elders gathered in spontaneous worship, prayer, and Spirit-guided response.

In the course of our free-flowing Scripture reading on our first night together, one pastor read the story of the ten lepers (see Luke 17:11-19). As I listened, I turned to the passage and prayed, and insight struck. Here was an occasion to pray in unity and application of the Word.

I told our leadership team, "These lepers knew their need. They understood the power of the One in their presence. They cried in desperation for His mercy." I continued with the application, "We, too, are people in need. We know there is One in our midst who has the power to show mercy, to heal, and to deliver. Perhaps we would want to cry out to Him with similar desperation."

I instructed the group, "One at a time, as the Spirit of God prompts us, let us finish this sentence: 'Jesus, I bring to You the leprosy of my (blank), and I cry out to You for healing.'" I then added, "After each person prays, let's all cry out in unison, as the lepers did, 'Jesus, Master, have mercy on us.'"

What followed was a powerful time of profound authenticity and creative confession. People were transparent about the "leprosies" of their hearts, relationships, and actions. The united sense of need for God's mercy in Christ was indeed a powerful, healing reality in our midst. Our hearts were humbled in powerful consideration of this holy healing grace. The loud, united, and repeated cry of our hearts, "Lord, Master, have mercy on us," still echoes in our hearts to this day. We also sprinkled this season of prayer with songs of confession and mercy.

As I sensed the group coming to a landing point for this focus, I journeyed on in the text to direct a second aspect of response. Here was a Samaritan, sensing his unworthiness, filled with genuine gratitude and returning to give thanks. Nine were healed of a physical affliction; one was made well. (Many commentators believe that this one man received the gift of eternal life as he moved beyond the physical healing to express real faith and recognition of Christ.)

I noted the actions of this Samaritan. He returned, he shouted, he fell face down and gave thanks for Christ's merciful healing power.

I urged these fellow leaders to join me in a season of offering similar thanks to Christ, considering all He has done in our lives. I said, "As you feel prompted, offer your thanks to Christ for what He has done in your life. Muster vocal energy as you do so. Let your body transmit what is in your soul. Maybe this will mean that you will fall on your face, or stand in praise, or humbly bow. But, in His presence, join with the Samaritan by praying, 'I praise You, Jesus, because You have healed me of . . .'" As we had done earlier, I asked the group to respond to each declaration with the united cry, "Give glory to God, your faith has made you well."

What followed was a Christ-honoring, cut-loose time of declaring the praise of our Savior. It was a faith-building, uniting season of powerful testimony and gratitude.

We closed the evening with some additional hymns and songs of praise. This marked the beginning of one of the most transforming prayer retreats I have ever experienced. We did not plan or script these moments.

Yet in this moment of PRAYzing! God opened the hearts of fellow leaders to Himself and to one another. This transparency, honesty, and praise did more to unite our leadership team than hundreds of hours in meetings and horizontal dialogue. When leaders "cry out" for mercy, then return to "shout out" in gratitude, it is good for the soul of the team and ultimately the soul of the church. In retrospect, we have all come to believe that this evening—and that retreat—marked the beginning of a new day for our relationships and the spiritual tone of our leadership in the church.

DECLARING HIS NAME

But You, O LORD, do not be far from Me;
O My Strength, hasten to help Me!
Deliver Me from the sword,
My precious life from the power of the dog.
Save Me from the lion's mouth
And from the horns of the wild oxen!
You have answered Me.
I will declare Your name to My brethren;
In the midst of the assembly I will praise You.
You who fear the LORD, praise Him!
All you descendants of Jacob, glorify Him,
And fear Him, all you offspring of Israel!
(PSALM 22:19-23)

For more than twenty years, I have led an early-morning prayer time on
Sunday mornings. This gathering serves as the first of several "powerhouse" prayer meetings held on Sunday mornings. Each is designed to
support the worship services and Sunday ministries through intercessory prayer but is still based in Scriptural worship.

Normally, I schedule this earliest prayer gathering to allow the worship pastors and other participants time afterward to prepare for ministry or to go back home to retrieve the family. In this case, we pray from 6:15 to 7:15 a.m.

Incidentally, I often recommend this to pastors as a great starting point for prayer ministry in the church. It is a great prayer routine because the pastor is desperate, with the services just around the corner. The people of the church seldom have conflicts early on a Sunday morning, and most are thinking about church that day. Personally, I have discovered some of my best insights for my already-prepared sermon during this prayer time as the Spirit applies the message to my own heart with freshness and as I hear the insightful prayers of God's people.

Each prayer time starts in a psalm. We simply journey through the psalms one at a time in sequential fashion. The profound discovery of prayer material in each psalm never ceases to amaze me.

One morning at 6:15, a group of about fifteen opened to Psalm 22. I had not even previewed the passage. After a careful group reading of the psalm, we began to worship in spontaneous song and reiteration of the truths of this passage. Even a casual reading will demonstrate this to be a messianic segment, giving us a glimpse of the struggle of Christ on the cross. The theme of the psalm is extreme suffering and trouble, trumped by the character and deliverance and praise of God.

As we prayed, my heart was drawn to verses 21 and 22: "You have answered Me. I will declare Your name to My brethren; in the midst of the assembly I will praise You." I knew that every person in the room had a lifelong track record of answered prayers that provided deeper understanding of the name and nature of the Lord. I wanted to make this practical in a way that would energize and unite our hearts. I instructed the group as we focused on these verses, "Let's take just a moment to respond in similar fashion. I want to ask each of you to declare His name with these words, 'Lord, I declare that Your name is (blank) because You have answered my prayer for (blank).'"

In spite of the early hour, vigor filled the room as we considered the Lord's name and previous answers to prayer. Examples included:

"Lord, I declare that Your name is holy because You have answered my prayer for pure eyes and a consecrated heart."

"Lord, I declare that Your name is Jehovah Jireh because You have answered my prayer for a job that provides for my needs."

"Lord, I declare that Your name is Prince of Peace because You have heard my prayer and healed the deep conflict in my marriage."

"Lord, I declare that You are the Gentle Shepherd because You have patiently directed my son back to Your heart and home to his family."

"Lord, I declare that You are the Author and Finisher of my faith because You never gave up on me when I was stuck in apathy and disobedience."

These prayers continued for ten minutes. Even though our time that morning was limited, the expressions were potent. As we concluded this prayer time, our intercession for the services that day was especially passionate. We remembered that the essence of Sunday mornings was "declaring His name" and giving Him praise in the "midst of the assembly."

ELIMINATION COMMUNION

When He had given thanks, He broke it and said, "Take, eat; this is My body which is broken for you; do this in remembrance of Me." In the same manner He also took the cup after supper, saying, "This cup is the new covenant in My blood. This do, as often as you drink it, in remembrance of Me."
(1 CORINTHIANS 11:24-25)

Therefore, my brethren, when you come together to eat, wait for one another.
(1 CORINTHIANS 11:33)

I have spent many years in churches that observed the Lord's Table every Sunday. On one hand, it was beautiful to place this powerful experience of remembrance central in the Sunday routine. But it often became just that: routine.

Whether you observe Communion weekly, monthly, quarterly, or in some sporadic pattern that is difficult to figure out, it is easy to get in a rut.

One year during an all-day staff retreat, we decided to celebrate Communion. I wanted it to be fresh and meaningful. In my heart, I felt we needed to encourage people to connect with the meaning of this commemoration while concurrently bonding with one another. PRAYzing! happened and we went on to experience a truly compelling remembrance of Christ, His work, and His call to live in vital community with one another.

I arranged the group in concentric circles around the elements. The bread and cup along with some candles sat on a beautifully draped table. We began by encouraging the group to read passages of Scripture related to the work of the Cross. This could include gospel narratives about Jesus on the cross, Old Testament prophecies about His saving work, or readings from the New Testament epistles teaching about His grace and sacrifice. We also encouraged spontaneous singing of choruses and hymns related to the cross. To assist in the singing, we had provided a book with lyrics to many of the songs.

After a season of worship, I asked everyone to stand. (I had preselected two others to assist me with the service.) Then I offered this instruction: "In just a moment, three of us are going to go to the table, pick up the bread and cup, then come to three of you. We will take a moment to explain the meaning of the bread and cup, seeking in our own words to express the love and grace of Christ that fills His heart for you. We will serve you the elements and then pause to pray a prayer of blessing on your life."

I continued, "Then we will ask those three to come to the table and repeat this approach with someone else. After you have *both* received and given Communion to someone, please sit down, indicating to us all that you have completed the process. This pattern will continue until everyone has been served and then had the occasion to serve someone else." Thus, one-by-one, participants would be "eliminated" from participating after they had completed the exercise.

After serving the first three, those of us who initiated the process went back to our seats and stood until we, too, were served. (However, we did have to monitor the flow, realizing that we might once again have to serve someone to keep the process moving along.) The group continued to sing songs and read Scripture during this exercise. Not only did it help keep the focus, it also allowed participants to interact in the Communion exchange without concern for everyone hearing what they were saying.

What ensued was a personal, encouraging, and fresh experience of the meaning of Communion. That tender moment of one-on-one explanation, followed by prayer, moved many to tears. The exercise not only strengthened the bond between staff members but also gave everyone a deeper appreciation of the practical power of the sacrificial death of our Savior.

FOOTSTOOL WORSHIP

Exalt the LORD our God,
And worship at His footstool —
He is holy.
(PSALM 99:5)

Thus says the LORD:
"Heaven is My throne,
And earth is My footstool.
Where is the house that you will build Me?
And where is the place of My rest?
For all those things My hand has made,
And all those things exist,"
Says the LORD.
"But on this one will I look:
On him who is poor and of a contrite spirit,
And who trembles at My word."
(ISAIAH 66:1-2)

It was the second evening of one of our men's prayer summits. We were enjoying a wonderful retreat of Bible reading, worship, and prayer after a full day of spiritual enrichment and fellowship. As usual, men spontaneously read Scripture and connected songs together in a wonderful flow of united pursuit of God.

As it turned out, a couple of men read Psalm 99. I am not sure if the second man just did not hear the first one read the passage or if his repetition was intentional. In any case, it became another occasion for PRAYzing!

The psalm begins with the declaration, "The Lord reigns." The rest of the psalm is an elaboration on what this means. Also, twice in the psalm the declaration is made, "Exalt the LORD our God, and worship at His footstool — He is holy."

I instructed the men to declare God's reign in their own lives by completing the sentence, "Lord, I declare Your reign over . . ." I encouraged them to make this a point of surrender to the Lordship of Christ by noting the issues, people, and struggles they wanted to yield to His loving and holy reign. After each man offered this affirmation, I asked the rest of the men to announce in unison, "Exalt the Lord our God and worship at His footstool. He is holy." (By the way, this always turns out to be a great way to get a group to memorize a passage of Scripture. By the time they have repeated it thirty times, they have it down!)

We blended this invigorating exercise with songs about God's reign and holiness. The men continued for about twenty minutes. In the midst of this time, I thought of Isaiah 66:1-2, which speaks more specifically of the Lord's footstool. Heaven is His throne, and earth is His footstool.

At this particular summit, we were in an astounding part of the "footstool," perched eight thousand feet above sea level at a beautiful campground beside a pristine alpine lake in the Sierra Nevada Mountains. Massive evergreens shot into the horizon, and the stars were more radiant than anything we had ever seen. It was a warm night with a clear sky.

As the responsive prayers began to subside, I read the Isaiah passage, noting that in spite of its magnitude and grandeur, our earth is but the footstool of God. The passage indicates that He is beyond the containment of any temple or construct of human effort. Yet, great and holy as He is, He longs to look (gaze with approval) upon the hearts of men. Isaiah indicated that He is especially pleased with those who are humble, are contrite in spirit, and tremble at His word.

I asked the men to join me in a "code of silence," which is a time of structured solitude without any interruption of talking. I encouraged the men to find a place somewhere alone under the stars and quietly worship at God's footstool. I further encouraged each man to ask this awesome God to give him a humble, broken heart that trembles at the truth of His Word.

Those forty-five minutes of contemplative worship, on the heels of such an invigorating experience of surrender and praise, literally changed lives. My own life was indelibly marked by that encounter at the "footstool" of the high, holy, and mighty Creator. A longing heart, before a holy God, with such a powerful visualization of His grandeur will result in a life of deeper declaration of His rule and reign over the universe and in our hearts.

GENERATION TO GENERATION

I will extol You, my God, O King;
And I will bless Your name forever and ever.
Every day I will bless You,
And I will praise Your name forever and ever.
Great is the LORD, and greatly to be praised;
And His greatness is unsearchable.
One generation shall praise Your works to another,
And shall declare Your mighty acts.
I will meditate on the glorious splendor of Your majesty,
And on Your wondrous works.
Men shall speak of the might of Your awesome acts,
And I will declare Your greatness.
They shall utter the memory of Your great goodness,
And shall sing of Your righteousness.
(PSALM 145:1-7)

One beautiful aspect of effective prayer is its transgenerational aspect. Over the years, saints from 18 to 81 have enjoyed unprecedented rich fellowship in the context of our prayer summits. After three days of Scripture reading, a cappella singing, honest sharing, supportive prayer, and authentic fellowship, the generational gap is bridged in ways beyond anything I have ever witnessed.

On one particular occasion, various Scriptures were read in the flow of worship and prayer about the "next generation." Psalm 145:1-7 especially caught my attention. The psalm expresses a resolve to praise the Lord for His greatness. I noticed the determination to speak of God's awesome acts, declare His greatness, and utter the memory of His goodness. The passage stated that one generation should praise His works to another. The Lord prompted me to pray in a way that would maximize the experience.

The room was filled with a mix of generations. I arbitrarily put the dividing line at forty years of age. Then I asked everyone over forty to consider the memory of God's works in their lives. The passage commanded the utterance of these acts of His greatness, so I asked each "older" person to consider a specific aspect of participation. I requested, "As you feel led, finish this sentence: 'In my generation, I have seen Your wondrous works in (of, by) . . .' and then finish the sentence with some specific but brief recollection of your experience of His power and goodness."

I then asked everyone under forty to respond in unison to each declaration with this echo: "We will meditate on Your glorious splendor and wondrous works." They understood, and they started. It was indeed glorious, wondrous, and awesome. Some examples were:

"In my generation, I have seen Your wondrous works as You have sustained our family through many financial crises."

"In my generation, I have seen Your wondrous works as You have brought hard-hearted family members to a saving knowledge of Christ."

"In my generation, I have seen Your wondrous works as You have sustained our family after the tragic death of my grandchild."

"In my generation, I have seen Your wondrous works as You have delivered my husband and my son from the bondage of substance abuse."

The echo of the younger crowd, "We will meditate on Your glorious splendor and wondrous works," made each reflection even more powerful. If God had been that good in the past, certainly He could be trusted for goodness in the present and the future.

The older generation was able to encourage the younger with their track record of experience with the goodness and awesome works of God. The younger crowd had the occasion to consider the greatness of God in specific ways. It was not only a faith-building experience but also a uniting encounter among generations often divided over superficial differences. In this moment, all chronological distinctions faded in light of the shared passion for the greatness of our very good God.

HALLELUJAH! PRAISE THE LORD!

Let everything that has breath praise the LORD.
Praise the LORD!
(PSALM 150:6)

Praise the LORD!
Praise the name of the LORD;
Praise Him, O you servants of the LORD!
You who stand in the house of the LORD,
In the courts of the house of our God,
Praise the LORD, for the LORD is good;
Sing praises to His name, for it is pleasant.
(PSALM 135:1-3)

And the twenty-four elders and the four living creatures fell
down and worshiped God who sits on the throne saying,
"Amen. Hallelujah!" And a voice came from the throne,
saying, "Give praise to our God, all you His bond-servants,
you who fear Him, the small and the great." Then I heard
something like the voice of a great multitude and like the
sound of many waters and like the sound of mighty peals of
thunder, saying,
"Hallelujah! For the Lord our God, the Almighty, reigns."
(REVELATION 19:4-6, NASB)

What human words are sufficient to express our overflowing praise for God's supernatural work in our lives? The commonly used biblical expressions are "Praise the Lord" and "Hallelujah." (Both are essentially synonymous and mean "Praise You, Jehovah.") Throughout the centuries of Jewish and Christian worship, these words have expressed joyous adoration for Jehovah God.

On a crisp, cool Minnesota morning, our church was concluding a three-day prayer summit that involved both men and women from the congregation. A couple dozen pastors and leaders from various parts of the country had also sat in with us to experience and learn from these days of transformation.

There seemed to be holy electricity in the room. Gratitude filled our hearts because of all that the Lord had accomplished during our time together. Songs of praise rang out. Someone started the old chorus, "How can I say thanks for the things you have done for me?" As we echoed our gratitude, those words stuck in my mind. How could we really say thanks?

I remembered someone reading previously from Psalms and Revelation, focusing on the declarations, "Praise the Lord" and "Hallelujah." It hit me. That is how we do it.

As that song ended, I spoke up and explained the plan. Psalm 135:3 (which someone had read earlier) states, "Praise the LORD, for the LORD is good." Then I asked, "How have you seen God's goodness in these past few days? How might you want to thank Him for His goodness, in specific terms, as you reflect on our time together?" Then I offered these instructions: "I want to ask some of you to stand and give God thanks for the ways you have seen and experienced His goodness. To affirm and participate fully in that moment, here is what we will do. After each declaration, I want to ask all the women to shout out, 'Hallelujah!' and the men to follow by shouting, 'Praise the Lord!'"

They got it.

Actually, this idea was reminiscent of a simple little song I used to enjoy in Sunday school with the girls singing, "Hallelu, hallelu, hallelu, hallelujah," and the boys responding, "Praise ye the Lord." Since the spirit of the group was already so joyful and enthusiastic, I figured this would be a good moment to try something a little out of the box.

So we started. Wow! It was like unleashing a herd of stallions. One person right after another exclaimed gratitude for a fresh sense of the goodness of God. Enthusiastic affirmation followed with a "Hallelujah!" (women) and "Praise the Lord!" (men).

I sat with my eyes closed the entire time, trying to soak it all in as I grinned from ear to ear. Suddenly, one of the visiting pastors, sitting next to me, tapped me on the shoulder and said, "Look up! They're doing the wave!" Sure enough, without my noticing, the women had started standing up with arms upraised shouting, "Hallelujah!" and then sitting down again. The men followed, in similar aerobic fashion, with a hearty "Praise the Lord!" It was quite a sight as unbridled joy exploded.

If you understand the typical reserved nature of Minnesota culture, you will identify with my surprise. Yet as I reflected on the texts that inspired this moment of celebration, I noted that one spoke of those who "stood in the house of the Lord" to declare their praise (see Psalm 135:2), while the other described the twenty-four elders who "fell down and worshiped" (Revelation 19:4). It is a stretch, but perhaps our "Minnesota wave" reflected a modern rendition of these physical responses of worship. In any case, it was a powerful conclusion to a profound experience of Christ's goodness in our midst.

ISAIAH'S CALL, OUR SURRENDER

In the year that King Uzziah died, I saw the Lord sitting on a
throne, high and lifted up, and the train of His robe filled the
temple. Above it stood seraphim; each one had six wings:
with two he covered his face, with two he covered his feet,
and with two he flew. And one cried to another and said:
"Holy, holy, holy is the Lord of hosts;
The whole earth is full of His glory!"
And the posts of the door were shaken by the voice of him
who cried out, and the house was filled with smoke.
So I said: "Woe is me, for I am undone!
Because I am a man of unclean lips,
And I dwell in the midst of a people of unclean lips;
For my eyes have seen the King,
The Lord of hosts."
Then one of the seraphim flew to me, having in his hand a
live coal which he had taken with the tongs from the altar.
And he touched my mouth with it, and said:
"Behold, this has touched your lips;
Your iniquity is taken away,
And your sin purged."
Also I heard the voice of the Lord, saying:
"Whom shall I send,
And who will go for Us?" Then I said, "Here am I! Send me."
(ISAIAH 6:1-8)

We came to the final session of a three-day prayer summit. Everyone's thoughts focused on the challenges of returning to home, work, school, and church. After these profound days of experiencing the treasure of Christ's presence, the joy of fellowship, and the cleansing of deep confession, I wondered, *What might the Lord want to say in these concluding moments?*

Knowing that prayer should not be a cul-de-sac of ingrown inspiration but a thoroughfare to more powerful ministry, I felt we needed to consider the practical impact of this mountaintop experience. I waited and listened for a passage of Scripture to provide the needed direction, trusting the Spirit to give me the right insight for application.

When someone read Isaiah 6:1-8, I sensed this was the right point of participation. Isaiah had just witnessed the abrupt death of King Uzziah when he violated the holiness of the temple of God and was stricken with leprosy. Isaiah understood the spiritual condition of the day and described himself as a man of unclean lips living among people who were likewise impure. In the midst of this, God gave him a profound experience of His holiness. Most of us have read it and felt the power of this Old Testament encounter. However, never before had I encountered the application of His holiness as I did at that moment in this prayer summit.

As we all prepared to depart this extraordinary prayer experience to go back to the homes, jobs, and challenges of daily life, Isaiah's encounter framed the moment for us so well.

I asked the group to cry out in unison, "Holy, Holy, Holy," to begin each cycle of prayer. Then I asked a man named Ed (who is now with the Lord) to represent the question and call of God to our hearts by crying out loudly and with authority, "Whom shall I send, and who will go for us?"

Finally, I asked the people around the room to respond one at a time, as prompted by the Spirit, "Here am I, Lord. Send me to (blank)." I instructed each person to consider the special challenges he or she faced after the summit. Their response would be a declaration to accept the call of a Holy God to the lives of people in need all around them. What occurred was one of the most powerful prayer experiences I have ever witnessed.

The flow went like this:

All: "Holy, Holy, Holy."
Ed: "Whom shall I send, and who will go for us?"
Individuals: "Here am I, Lord. Send me to . . ."

This responsive cycle of praise, inquiry, and response continued for about thirty minutes. Men and women were declaring their trust in a Holy God as He sent them back to an unsaved coworker, a difficult marriage, a wandering child, a struggling ministry, a dead-end job, a dying parent, a financial crisis, and a new sense of calling. The list of needs, trials, and opportunities went on and on. Tears flowed freely. The glory of the Lord filled the temple of our gathering. When it was over, we all stood in awe of a holy and powerful God whose calling would be accompanied by His enabling grace to accomplish His will. We closed with a flow of songs about His holiness and power. At the end, we gathered close in the middle of the room, standing arm in arm and singing a final round of "Shine, Jesus, Shine." Our hearts were full and fully prepared to take His life to the waiting world as representatives of His grace and glory.

J

JESUS, MY BIOGRAPHY

Because as He is, so are we in this world.
(1 JOHN 4:17)

For whom He foreknew, He also predestined to be
conformed to the image of His Son, that He might be the
firstborn among many brethren.
(ROMANS 8:29)

Approximately a hundred men and women sat in concentric circles in
the large meeting room. We had gathered for another prayer summit
and were enjoying a morning session with no agenda, marked by free-
flowing praise, Scripture reading, and prayer.

The theme of Christlikeness emerged in the various Scripture readings and songs. As I contemplated the idea, the thought struck me that
if we are to be like Christ, then, when it is all said and done, His life and
character should be our biography. First John 4:17 declares, "as He is, so
are we in this world."

I paused to explain this idea, reiterating the many verses that had marked this season of worship and prayer. Then I asked the group to turn to the Gospels to consider some of the accounts of Jesus' life, ministry, and teaching. I asked people to begin to read some of these accounts, slowly and thoughtfully. After each reading, I asked the group to respond with a collective prayer, "Jesus, be my biography."

What followed was an hour of profound insight into our Lord. Our collective cry, "Jesus, be my biography," grew more passionate and tender as we went. It became one of the most practical calls to Christlikeness any of us had ever experienced.

After the retreat, one of the young men (Jonathan Stone, who is now a missionary in Africa) wrote a two-part reading to accurately capture the power of this moment. He still credits this PRAYzing! experience as catalytic to his call to missions.

The following Sunday at church, two young men recited the reading. The impact was profound.

VOICE 1	VOICE 2
Jesus, be my biography	
What is Your name?	
	My name is Jesus
	I AM
	I am.
Jesus	Jesus
Worthy is Your name	
Jesus	Jesus
You are the Rock	
You are the Good Shepherd	
Jesus	Jesus
What is Your biography?	
	I am Love
Love produces fruit in us	
	The fullness of God is in Me

VOICE 1	VOICE 2
	The greatness of God
What a contrast of our sinful nature!	
Jesus	Jesus
We are about the business of	I am about the business of
Jesus	You
	I am the Christ
	I am the Precious Cornerstone
	I am the Firstborn over all Creation
	I am the One who loved you so much
	That I died for you
On a cross	On a cross
Jesus, let me take up Your cross	
	I was an ugly sacrifice
It is hard to look at the blood	
	I was rejected and mocked
It is hard to recognize You	
	I was pierced with nails and thorns
It is hard to see Your face	
Seek Your face	Seek My face
Even when I compromise the Truth	
	I keep My word
When I am broken	
	I wipe away your tears
When I waste what You have given me	
	I restore My creation
When I am dry and withered	
	I renew your life
When I feel inadequate	
	I am able to do immeasurably more
	than you ever think or imagine

VOICE 1	VOICE 2
When I am dead	
	I am the Resurrection and the Life
Jesus	Jesus
	Listen to My biography
Jesus, be my biography	
Listen	Listen
	I am Self-Existent
All this creation could not exist without You?	
Listen	Listen
The silent wind moves	
	In the arching grasses I whisper
The smooth waves ripple	
	In the lapping waters I speak
The tender trees wait	
	In the octaves of the branches I sing
Listen	Listen
The Lord doesn't need this creation to exist	
But listen, it's proclaiming all around you.	
Listen	Listen
An ant's footsteps across a path	
	Listen
A woodpecker's rhythm on a tree	
	Listen
A songbird's laugh of pure melody	
	Listen
An echoing cry of a loon	
	Listen
Can you see it?	
	Can you hear it?
Self-Existent One	Self-Existent One

VOICE 1	VOICE 2
Transcendent	Transcendent
Elohim Creator	Elohim Creator
You are	I AM
	It is enough
To worship You my	
King	King
Faithful	King
Trustworthy	King
Good	King
No treason in my heart	
No declaration of independence from You	
You are my	
King	King of Israel
You are my	
King	King of the Jews
You are my	
King	King of the Ages
You are my self-sufficient	
King	King of Kings and Lord of Lords
I come before You with a broken heart	
	My grace is sufficient for you
	Enter My innermost chamber
	Come and have intimacy
With a King?	
	Trust Me
	I know you completely
I am broken completely	
I lay out my heart before the King	King of Refuge
	You are safe in the shelter of My wings
	You are protected in the refuge of My

VOICE 1	VOICE 2
Walls	Walls
Of protection	
Walls	Walls
Of Jerusalem	
Walls	Walls of
Firewall	Fire
	Put on your armor
Truth	Truth
	On your waist
Righteousness	Righteousness
	On your chest
Peace	Peace
	On your feet
Salvation	Salvation
	On your head
Faith	Faith
	As a shield before you
The Spirit	The Spirit
	As your sword
	Now walk
Step by step	
In Your Greatness	In My greatness
Jesus, be my biography	Jesus, be my biography

K

KING JESUS, HERE'S MY CROWN

His eyes were like a flame of fire, and on His head were many crowns. He had a name written that no one knew except Himself. He was clothed with a robe dipped in blood, and His name is called The Word of God. And the armies in heaven, clothed in fine linen, white and clean, followed Him on white horses. Now out of His mouth goes a sharp sword, that with it He should strike the nations. And He Himself will rule them with a rod of iron. He Himself treads the winepress of the fierceness and wrath of Almighty God. And He has on His robe and on His thigh a name written: KING OF KINGS AND LORD OF LORDS.
(REVELATION 19:12-16)

The twenty-four elders fall down before Him who sits on the throne and worship Him who lives forever and ever, and cast their crowns before the throne, saying:
"You are worthy, O Lord,
To receive glory and honor and power;
For You created all things,
And by Your will they exist and were created."
(REVELATION 4:10-11)

Few titles are more inspiring than the one given to Jesus alone, "King of kings." He is worthy to sit on the throne ruling the universe. He is worthy to wear His many crowns. Someday we will each have the joy of casting our crowns of reward before His throne, adding the honors of our earthly service to the glory of His eternal reign.

More than once, these truths have become the centerpiece of our focus and worship in collective gatherings of prayer. Never has this captivation been more powerful than at a pastors' prayer summit I was leading for a group of churches in the upper Midwest.

These leaders had experienced a powerful movement of unity and humility in their city. Weekly they gathered to pray for one another and ask God's blessing on the gospel-preaching churches of the area. Eventually, the momentum of their spiritual pursuit led them to sponsor a two-day prayer summit. I was honored with the invitation to lead this gathering. This occasion of PRAYzing! occurred at our second annual summit and truly touched us all at a deep level.

Our worship had again centered on the rule of King Jesus. In these moments of focus, a pastor read of the day when we will cast our crowns at Jesus' feet, giving Him all the glory for everything He accomplished in and through us in this life. The Spirit prompted me to park on that thought, giving guidance to what proved to be a very meaningful prayer exercise.

As we continued in prayer, I directed individual leaders to consider the specific things the Lord had accomplished in their lives or through their ministries. Then I requested that we all use our imagination to picture that day when we will cast our crowns at the throne of the King. I gave these instructions: "As you feel led, I want each of you to come to the middle of our circle of chairs and kneel there, as if before His throne, and declare, 'King Jesus, I look forward to the day when I can cast before You my crown of (blank).'" Then I asked each to symbolically lay that crown down before the King.

Eagerly, these pastors and many of their spouses began to respond.

After each expression of demonstrative, humble worship, we all echoed, "King of kings and Lord of lords." What a powerful moment. Pastors imagined the joy of casting before the Lord the crowns of their growing ministries, evangelistic impact, healthy families, spiritually attuned children, faithful devotions, well-delivered sermons, successful counseling impact, theological education, effective spiritual gifts—their entire lives. They knelt in humble adoration. The list of "crowns" was diverse, practical, and deeply meaningful.

The Lord must have received special pleasure as these ministry leaders, often recognized and respected by others, eagerly longed for the day when the King would receive all the glory for everything that had been done in His name. As we concluded this segment with choruses of "All Hail King Jesus," "Majesty," and "All Hail the Power of Jesus' Name," everyone felt a fresh sense of perspective about the meaning and reward of our ministries for the sake of the gospel.

LOVED, EVEN WHEN . . .

The LORD has appeared of old to me, saying:
"Yes, I have loved you with an everlasting love;
Therefore with lovingkindness I have drawn you."
(JEREMIAH 31:3)

He who does not love does not know God, for God is love. In this the love of God was manifested toward us, that God has sent His only begotten Son into the world, that we might live through Him.
(1 JOHN 4:8-9)

It was one of my very first prayer summit experiences. About 150 men and women gathered in the large meeting room at Richardson Springs retreat center near Chico, California. As has often become the case, the morning session included segments of Scripture reading, spontaneous singing, and an effort to discover particular themes for our group focus.

At a particular moment, the focus of our reading began to center on the love of God. Hymns and choruses flowed from our hearts as we considered the magnitude of God's love in Christ.

I took the occasion to reflect on His unfailing love as I directed the group, still in a spirit of prayer. I explained that God loves us not because of who we are but because of who He is. It is His character to love His children. His choice, not our performance, is the basis of His deep love for us. I helped the participants understand that we will never do anything to prompt God to love us any more and cannot do anything to cause Him to love us any less.

With that, the Spirit prompted me to lead people to pray in a way that would make this truth specific and dynamic. I asked those who felt led to finish the sentence in the form of a prayer of gratitude: "Lord, I praise You that You love me even if (or even when) . . ." After each personal expression of thanksgiving, I instructed the rest of the group to declare the simple lyric from the song, "Oh, How He Loves You and Me."

The prayers flowed freely in honest, heartfelt sentences like these:

"Lord, I thank You that You love me even when my disobedience breaks Your heart."

"Lord, thank You that You love me even when I am a disappointment to other people."

"Lord, I thank You that You love me even when I am not considered a success by the standards of this world."

"Lord, I thank You that You love me even when my spouse has rejected me and left me for another lover."

"Lord, I thank You that You love me even if I never measure up to the unrealistic expectations my parents have for my life."

The healing and liberating power of the love of God in Christ was on splendid display that morning. The Lord delivered hearts from the "performance-based acceptance" treadmill. Some felt God's love at a deeper level than ever before. Some declared His love with tears, others with joy—all with passion. The power of God's love in providing acceptance and responsive obedience is very real. I cannot remember it being any more real in the experience of a group than it was on that morning of tender worship.

M

MAJESTY IN OUR MIDST

The LORD reigns, He is clothed with majesty;
The LORD is clothed,
He has girded Himself with strength.
Surely the world is established, so that it cannot be moved.
(PSALM 93:1)

. . . but were eyewitnesses of His majesty. For He received
from God the Father honor and glory.
(2 PETER 1:16-17)

I will meditate on the glorious splendor of Your majesty,
And on Your wondrous works.
Men shall speak of the might of Your awesome acts,
And I will declare Your greatness.
They shall utter the memory of Your great goodness,
And shall sing of Your righteousness.
(PSALM 145:5-7)

Sometimes PRAYzing! happens when you least expect it. The worship
service was midstream. We clipped off the opening remarks, offering, and announcements. The sermon was next on the agenda as the

congregation for our second service, some 2,300 strong, stood in passionate song.

At this moment when my mind was typically engaged in a fusion of mental activity (sermon note review, watching the lyrics on the screen, and trying to hit the right notes), something different was occurring. I wept as the words began to resonate in the depths of my being.

The song spoke of being humbled in the presence of His Majesty and moved by His sacrificial death on our behalf. Themes of His great love, forgiveness, and grace punctuated the lyrics and penetrated my heart. As we sang the word "Majesty" over and over again, I sensed this was a PRAYzing! moment. At the Spirit's prompting, I went to the front, signaled my worship pastor that I would like to interrupt, and asked the congregation:

"What would we do if the president of the United States and his entourage of bodyguards and assistants walked into the worship center right now? How would we respond?"

"More important, what would we do if the resurrected Christ suddenly appeared before our physical eyes, as He did for John in Revelation 1? Would it be just another Sunday of perfunctory worship?"

"What will we do when we stand in His holy presence in the company of all the saints and angels of heaven? We are in His presence. He is here in our midst. So, whatever we think we will do on that day, let us do it right now."

The people understood the questions and the instruction. While I did not suggest anything in particular, it was clear that the Spirit was letting everyone know what He had in mind. It was a remarkable sight. Young and old alike responded with immediate sensitivity but profound diversity. Some stood in rapt attention, staring to the sky as if looking at the Savior's face. Others sat, face in hands, projecting a humble heart. Some maneuvered between the theater-style seats and knelt in reverence. Many stood with hands up, stretched in passionate praise. The aisles filled with people stepping outside the seating area to find a place to bow. I was told that many lay prostrate on the carpet in abandonment before His holy presence.

Personally, I witnessed none of this. Others described the response to me later. I had already walked to a quiet corner of the stage and was facedown in His presence.

I understand that the worship team on the platform reflected similar freedom as those in the pews. Tears flowing, our worship pastor fell to his knees to lead the congregation in a few more choruses of the song, followed by passionate prayers of confession and worship.

It was a holy moment, a timeless moment. We could not afford to interrupt the carefully scripted service plan but learned that we could not afford to miss moments like this. That day will forever be etched in our minds as an occasion when we got beyond the predesigned details of the service to encounter Christ in the service.

NAMES OF GOD, HEARTS OF TRUST

And those who know Your name will put their trust in You;
For You, LORD, have not forsaken those who seek You.
(PSALM 9:10)

And in His name Gentiles will trust.
(MATTHEW 12:21)

The essential tool for effective worship-based prayer is a copy of Scripture. As Psalm 40:7 states, "Behold, I come; in the scroll of the book it is written of me." Jesus reaffirmed this with His words, "You search the Scriptures, for in them you think you have eternal life; and these are they which testify of Me" (John 5:39). Every prayer meeting I lead starts with an open Bible.

Another practical tool for dynamic prayer times is a listing of the names and attributes of God. We often provide such a list in our various prayer times. We always include it in the guidebook for our three-day prayer summits. In fact, we have descriptions of God's attributes along with the listings and associated Scripture passages for the names of the Father, the Son, and the Holy Spirit.

More than once, we have used these lists for powerful united seasons of prayer. I often say that worship is the response of all I am to the revelation of all He is. Knowing God's name and character is the foundation of real worship.

On one particular occasion, a participant at one of our prayer meetings read from Psalm 9. One of the most beloved verses from the psalm is verse 10: "Those who know Your name will put their trust in You."

Prompted by the Spirit, I wanted those in our prayer gathering to experience the power of this verse. With the list of the names of God on hand, we broke into groups of five or six, and I asked each person to review that list and then pray this simple prayer: "Lord, because Your name is (blank), I will trust You for (blank)." I encouraged each one to consider the meaning of the names of God and the impact that truth will have on their ability to trust Him.

The groups buzzed with tender and specific prayers of confidence in God. God's character prompted individuals to trust Him for some very real, practical, and sometimes painful issues in life.

After about fifteen minutes, we transitioned with a verse and chorus of "'Tis So Sweet to Trust in Jesus." I kept the participants in their small groups and once again referenced Psalm 9 with a focus on verse 9: "The LORD also will be a refuge for the oppressed, a refuge in times of trouble." We also considered the promise of verse 12: "He does not forget the cry of the humble."

We sang a verse of the related hymn "Pass Me Not, O Gentle Savior, Hear My Humble Cry." I then asked participants to intercede for one another, asking the Lord to prove Himself to be a refuge to each one who offered a humble cry of trust in His name.

After another ten minutes of heartfelt intercession, we closed in song with an upbeat round of "No Other Name but the Name of Jesus."

After the first time through the song, we stopped and I asked everyone to fire off some of those names once again. The room was filled with affirmations and "Amens." We closed by repeating the song once more and left the room with fresh trust in the great names of our God.

OPEN HANDS, GRATEFUL HEARTS

These all wait for You,
That You may give them their food in due season.
What You give them they gather in;
You open Your hand, they are filled with good.
(PSALM 104:27-28)

You open Your hand
And satisfy the desire of every living thing.
(PSALM 145:16)

We approached the conclusion of another fabulous three-day prayer summit. Every heart was filled with the joy of the Lord and a profound sense of His personal work in each life. A variety of free-flowing songs rose from our hearts, punctuated with spontaneous Scripture reading. It seemed that this format was as fresh at that moment as it had been the night we began the summit earlier in the week.

Much of our praying during these days had focused on seeking God's face, not His hand. The face of God represents who He is—His character and glory. The hand of God speaks of what He does—His provision and acts of intervention. I often say that if we seek only His hand, we may miss His face. But if we seek His face, He is glad to open His hand.

People "happened" to read some verses back-to-back that spoke of God's hand. I was struck by the truth of Psalm 145:16 and paused to ask the reader to repeat the verse several times. As she did, the prayer application was obvious.

In reflecting on the many blessings of these days of worship, prayer, and fellowship, I commented on how the Lord had satisfied the deep needs and longings of our hearts, as only He can do. I repeated the verse again: "You open Your hand and satisfy the desire of every living thing." Then I suggested, "Let's take some time to thank the Lord for the satisfaction He has accomplished in us by opening His hand of provision. Who would finish the sentence, 'Lord, You have opened Your hand and satisfied my desire for . . .'?"

As we often do, I encouraged a group response, taking my cue from Psalm 104:28, "You open Your hand, they are filled with good." I asked the group to echo a response by saying, "And we are filled with good!"

It took off immediately. People cried out:

"Lord, You have opened Your hand and satisfied my desire for forgiveness."

"Lord, You have opened Your hand and satisfied my desire for acceptance."

"Lord, You have opened Your hand and satisfied my desire for renewed joy."

"Lord, You have opened Your hand and satisfied my desire for peace."

The responses were as personal and unique as the depths of each heart. We were amazed at the power of God's hand to minister satisfaction in such practical ways. With deep enthusiasm, we were able to echo, "And we are filled with good!"

Indeed we were.

POTTER

But now, O LORD,
You are our Father;
We are the clay, and You our potter;
And all we are the work of Your hand.
(ISAIAH 64:8)

The word which came to Jeremiah from the LORD, saying:
"Arise and go down to the potter's house, and there I will
cause you to hear My words." Then I went down to the
potter's house, and there he was, making something at the
wheel. And the vessel that he made of clay was marred
in the hand of the potter; so he made it again into another
vessel, as it seemed good to the potter to make. Then the
word of the LORD came to me, saying: "O house of Israel,
can I not do with you as this potter?" says the LORD. "Look,
as the clay is in the potter's hand, so are you in My hand, O
house of Israel!"
(JEREMIAH 18:1-6)

Many powerful moments of creative, breakthrough prayer have occurred in small groups. The large-group parts of the prayer summits
are stimulating and full of PRAYzing! Yet we always sense the need for

occasions when men can gather with men, and women with women, in groups of twenty or so as a vital extension of worship and prayerful response.

As we read the Word and worship God, I've watched men get gut-level honest with Him and one another about the real and deep issues of life. As James says, "Confess your trespasses to one another, and pray for one another, that you may be healed. The effective, fervent prayer of a righteous man avails much" (5:16). The stories are countless and glorious. Most are too personal to share in this book.

On one such occasion, the Lord led us to focus on His role as the "Potter" over our lives. This led to some engaging moments of creative, responsive prayer that ministered deeply to each heart. As we considered the truths of Jeremiah 18, one man read from the *New Living Translation*, which says,

> The jar he was making did not turn out as he had hoped, so [the potter] squashed the jar into a lump of clay and started again. Then the LORD gave me this message: "O Israel, can I not do to you as this potter has done to his clay? As the clay is in the potter's hand, so are you in my hand." (verses 4-6)

We made this passage our prayer focus. We placed a chair in the middle of the circle and invited each man to come and pour out his heart in response to the conviction of the Holy Spirit, but only as he felt led. Over time, men came, freely opening the clay of their hearts to the clear, tender reconstruction work of the Potter. After every prayer, a few others would gather to intercede on behalf of that brother.

One after another, men came to the chair to confess the ways in which the clay of their lives had disappointed the Potter. We used a simple pattern, "Lord, my life has not turned out as You wanted because the clay of my heart has become hardened by the sin of (blank)." Others prayed, "Lord the clay of my life is full of lumps of (blank)." Most of these prayers were followed by a risky but sincere invitation for the Lord to squash pride and resistance and start over as He wished.

Usually each season of confession, restoration, and intercession on behalf of an individual was followed by a song of recommitment and dedication. The afternoon flew by so quickly as God conducted intimate and remarkable renewal in our midst. These occasions seem so rare in the church today, but the Word and Spirit are still and always available to bring us to cleansing and restoration as we take time to wait on Him and pray for one another.

QUIET LESSONS

My soul, wait silently for God alone,
For my expectation is from Him.
(PSALM 62:5)

Be still, and know that I am God;
I will be exalted among the nations,
I will be exalted in the earth!
(PSALM 46:10)

Recently, I sat in a quaint coffee shop in Waconia, Minnesota, working on this book. A large plaque on the adjacent wall caught my attention. It read, "Go placidly amid the noise and the haste, and remember what peace there may be in silence." Immediately, I recognized the truism as the opening line of a piece of poetry called "Desiderata," by Max Ehrmann. I still remember listening to a recording of it on an old 45 record as a teenager.

The peace of silence can actually be a powerful experience of PRAYzing! Over the years, I've watched this happen many times in a variety of prayer gatherings.

Very often during our three-day prayer summits, we sense the need to send participants away for a "code of silence." Individuals are encouraged to take their Bibles, the devotional material we provide, a songbook, and some journal pages to a quiet place where they can enjoy the spiritual disciplines of solitude and silence, typically for a period of forty-five minutes to an hour. Without fail, these moments are the most profound experiences of the summit.

Silence allows for reflection on Scripture, songs, and themes of a recent group session. It provides a moment to simply "be" rather than "do." Silence gives the soul time to catch up to itself. In silence we experience the power of Psalm 46:10, "Cease striving and know that I am God" (NASB). Other translastions say to "be still" or "let go" or "relax." Don't we all need some doses of the vital experience of silence?

Over the years, participants have given their lives to Christ during the code of silence. Major spiritual breakthoughs have occurred in a hard heart. Clear direction has emerged for a life previously confused by the noise of the daily grind.

While Spirit-guided creativity can often lead to lively, high-energy experiences, it can also result in quiet moments of profound communion between the solitary soul and the Lord God Almighty.

One of the definitions of "zing" is "active strength of body or mind." There is an active strength in quietness. Synonyms of "zing" include fervor, life, passion, spirit, vigor, and vitality. Silence before God can restore all of these to the heart and mind. So, in the course of experiencing the creative leadership of the Spirit in prayer, take some time to quiet the soul, remembering what peace there can be in silence.

R

REMEMBER YOUR GREAT MOMENTS

I will remember the works of the LORD;
Surely I will remember Your wonders of old.
I will also meditate on all Your work,
And talk of Your deeds.
Your way, O God, is in the sanctuary;
Who is so great a God as our God?
(PSALM 77:11-13)

I remember the days of old;
I meditate on all Your works;
I muse on the work of Your hands.
I spread out my hands to You;
My soul longs for You like a thirsty land.
(PSALM 143:5-6)

Sometimes the truth of one simple sentence can radically impact the considerations of the heart and alter the course of a life. That has been the case for me, as I have often pondered the statement made in one of my seminary classes by a visiting Nazarene evangelist. Someone asked him the key to knowing God's will. His response was simple and direct. It has become profound in my life. He stated, "Learn to trust your great moments."

Behind that idea is the belief that God is always at work in our lives. We must consider that work, take note of it, and learn the lesson. By recording those truths, we can remember and trust the work of God from previous days as we chart our course in the present.

I've observed this principle in the feasts of Israel as the people remembered the works and character of God (see Exodus 12:14-20, 42). The twelve memorial stones gathered by Israel after crossing the Jordan River were designed to help God's people trust their great moments (see Joshua 4:7). The New Testament call to observe the Lord's Supper represents the same idea (see 1 Corinthians 11:23-26).

The way I do this in my life is through journaling. If you are going to trust your great moments, you had better have a very good memory or a faithful habit of writing things down. In countless ways, my recordings of God's work in my life have come into play as I consider the choices before me on the road of life.

As it relates to prayer, this idea has proven to be a powerful component in preserving the lasting impact of extraordinary moments in the presence of God. It has been especially helpful in capturing the lessons of prayer summits.

At many summits, I teach on the concept of trusting your great moments through "memorials." Since so many great moments occur when we give the Lord our undivided attention over an extended period, this component is essential.

Very often toward the end of a summit, we send participants off to spend an hour alone with the Lord and consider how they are going to memorialize and recall the spiritual breakthroughs and lessons that have occurred. Many will simply journal their reflections; others practice a little more "zing" and get creative.

Some have collected rocks or sticks, most of which they have inscribed with a verse. A few get serious and place this memorial on the floor next to their bed at night so it is the first thing they step on in the morning when they rise. Then they place it on the pillow during the day so as they lie down at night, it reminds them again. That is a serious desire to remember.

I know others who have made crosses and other symbols from a variety of materials. One man drove a large nail into a tree and came back to it every year to remember the issues he had "nailed down" with the Lord. The creative stories abound.

The lesson is simple: When God gives you "zing," place value in remembering. The lessons will last a lifetime and give you the guidance you need when you are tempted to doubt in the darkness what God has previously revealed to you in His light.

SHOUT TO GOD

Be glad in the LORD and rejoice, you righteous;
And shout for joy, all you upright in heart!
(PSALM 32:11)

Make a joyful shout to God, all the earth!
Sing out the honor of His name;
Make His praise glorious.
Say to God,
"How awesome are Your works!"
(PSALM 66:1-3)

Let us come before His presence with thanksgiving;
Let us shout joyfully to Him with psalms.
(PSALM 95:2)

At one men's prayer summit, we were taken by surprise as the Spirit of God took the Word of God and directed us to an expression of praise that was new to us all. As I listened to the men read a variety of Bible passages, one after another, I sensed an obvious theme. In each case, the verses spoke of "shouting to God."

It was clear to me that we were to put this biblical expression into practice even though this was completely new territory. By faith, I spoke up and directed the men: "I have never done this before, but it is obvious that the Lord is weaving a theme here." I instructed the men to stand, one at a time (as each felt prompted), and shout with all their might as they finished this sentence: "I shout to You, O God, because . . ."

One verse we had read previously was Psalm 66:3. I told the men that after each individual shouted in praise to God, we would all echo with united voices, "How awesome are Your works, O God!" After a chorus of the song "Shout to the Lord," the singing subsided and the shouting began.

What happened next was incredible. One after another, men would stand and cut loose with a passionate shout of praise to God. One man cried out, "I shout to You, O God, because Your love is better than life." Another man stood and exclaimed, "I shout to You, O God, because there is no condemnation for those who are in Christ Jesus." And another, "I shout to You, O God, because You have given me a new love for my wife." Of course, after each declaration, the remaining two hundred men raised their voices, "How awesome are Your works, O God." Laughter and hearty "Amens" seasoned the experience. The men clearly did not want to stop.

About forty-five minutes into this extraordinary expression of prayer and worship, one man cried out, "I shout to You, O God, because this is more fun than an NBA basketball game." (Indeed, it was!) At that, all the men burst into joyful laughter. It seemed like a good point to close.

We were overflowing with profound joy. These boisterous recollections of the power, promises, goodness, and provision of God had stimulated unprecedented gratitude, deeper faith, and an appreciation for fresh, biblical expressions of prayer.

As the night ended, the men were hoarse but amazed with this surprising experience of sincere joy. As a traditional church, it was quite a remarkable sight. Months later, most of us agree that our holy shouting match was one of the highlights of our many prayer summits and our Christian experience.

In a culture where so much of our worship looks like a cookie-cutter formula of mutual conformity, this evening of surprising but orderly shouts reminded us that our Father appreciates sincere and diverse worship in His holy presence.

TAKE OFF YOUR SHOES!

Then He said, "Do not draw near this place. Take your
sandals off your feet, for the place where you stand is
holy ground."
(EXODUS 3:5)

Then the Commander of the LORD's army said to Joshua,
"Take your sandal off your foot, for the place where you
stand is holy." And Joshua did so.
(JOSHUA 5:15)

We were midstream in an afternoon session at a recent all-church prayer
summit. As sometimes happens, the momentum seemed to wane a bit,
and I sensed it was time for a transition of focus or format. Nothing
was really coming to me, so I prayed for wisdom and insight. I needed
a fresh dose of PRAYzing!

I listened as people seemed to focus on passages about the holiness
of God. Someone started the song "Holy, Holy, Holy." Still, nothing
was coming to me. Suddenly, one of my cofacilitators thrust an open

page of our summit booklet from the chair behind me where he was sitting. I looked at the paper. It contained an image of clip art that said, "Take off your sandals, for the place where you stand is holy." He thumped the graphic with his finger as if the message was supposed to be clear. I prayed even more desperately for insight.

As they started the last verse of the hymn, PRAYzing! struck. Why did Moses (and later Joshua) have to take his shoes off in the presence of God's holiness? It occurred to me that it was because their shoes were dirty from the soil of their journey.

As the song ended, I carefully explained this insight and then offered direction to the group:

> Each of us is wearing shoes. These shoes represent where we have been lately in our lives. They have accumulated dirt from the journey. What dirt—what sin, what disobedience, what worry, what relational strain—might your shoes represent? In a moment, I want us to sing that first verse of "Holy, Holy, Holy" once again. After we are finished, I wonder if some of us might take off our shoes and bring them to the center of the room. As you lay them down there, consider a prayer like this: "Lord, in response to Your holiness, I take off my shoes of (blank)."

I went on to remind the group that we were in a mixed-gender context and to be discreet about their response. I knew this was a risk. To walk to the middle of a room, surrounded by over a hundred other people, and confess the "dirt" of your shoes was quite a challenge. Yet as the song ended, a dear woman stepped quietly to the center of the circle, weeping quietly. She prayed, "Lord, in response to Your holiness, I take off my shoes of worry about my wandering son." Spontaneously, someone called out "Holy, Holy, Holy." This became our group affirmation after each shoe removal.

The movement continued as people took off their shoes in the presence of a holy God, confessing worry, doubt, lack of faith, sinful attitudes, greed, envy, unforgiveness, gossip, pride, a spirit of competition, lack of love, and so on. Honestly, this astounding response lasted at least thirty minutes. The pile of shoes was significant, as you might imagine.

Then one of our pastors, whose shoes were already on the pile, came and lay down on the shoes. He wept openly as he cried out, "Lord, You already have my shoes. Here is my body. I give it to You as a living sacrifice. I confess the sins of our church. Forgive our pride, our arrogance, our denial. Humble us to fear You. We rend our hearts, not just our clothes. I repent and seek Your restoration." As he went on in some more specific ways, the weeping was noticeable all around the circle. I had just encountered one of the holiest moments of my life.

Other already-shoeless saints came and knelt in the middle, one at a time as the conviction and cleansing continued. It was obvious, as the prayers subsided, that the Lord was done working among us in this way.

We closed the afternoon with spontaneous prayers for individuals, families, pastors, and our church. A spirit of joy prevailed, as we all knew what David meant when he wrote, "Oh, what joy for those whose rebellion is forgiven, whose sin is put out of sight! Yes, what joy for those whose record the LORD has cleared of sin, whose lives are lived in complete honesty!" (Psalm 32:1-2, NLT).

U

UNEXPECTED RECONCILIATION

"And he will turn
The hearts of the fathers to the children,
And the hearts of the children to their fathers."
(MALACHI 4:6)

And you, fathers, do not provoke your children to wrath,
but bring them up in the training and
admonition of the Lord.
(EPHESIANS 6:4)

We were ready to start the afternoon session of a men's prayer summit at Lake Geneva Conference Center in Alexandria, Minnesota. The 175 men began to gather in the large assembly room. This was the very first summit experience for virtually every guy, as I had been at the church for only a couple months.

Originally, the men's committee had earmarked these dates for a typical men's retreat with a speaker, a worship leader, and lots of free time. During the process of my interviews as their candidate for senior pastor, they heard about this "prayer summit" experience. I found out that they immediately scrapped "Plan A" and reformatted everything to allow for this unprecedented prayer experience. I did not ask or expect them to do this, but I was glad they did.

In the minds of some, the jury was still out as to the real value and impact of this unusual format. Still, we were plodding along, reading Scripture, lifting our voices in praise, and waiting on the Lord with no agenda.

Because they had already secured a worship leader for the "retreat," we blended a little bit of scripted music in with the spontaneous singing. (Normally, everything is done a cappella.) The worship leader was not sure how to start. He mentioned that he had a song he was thinking of singing along with an accompaniment track. I cannot remember the title, but it had something to do with the Father's love.

Honestly, I was not very excited about the idea of a solo with a taped track, but he seemed enthused, so I gave him the go-ahead. I was about to learn once again that the Spirit can use all kinds of methods and formats to accomplish His purposes. He conducts His holy interruptions by His will and in His timing.

Some men were straggling in late from lunch, but by the time the song ended, most everyone had found a place. The song was good. In fact, the singer became noticeably choked up in the process of finishing the tune. During the song, the Spirit of God really put it on my heart to focus on the "Father" theme immediately.

I took a moment to talk about the need for the love of a father, especially The Father. Another cofacilitator spoke up about the wounds many men carry from their upbringing and the painful words or actions by their fathers. We began to worship in word and song around the theme of the mercy and grace of our Father God.

Before we knew it, this led to men turning to one another in spontaneous prayer, crying out for reconciliation and freedom as it related to some of their issues with "Dad" or as a dad. I watched as a silver-haired man, probably in his sixties, walked resolutely from one side of the room to the opposite corner. He took a young man in his arms. They embraced and visibly shook as each wept freely.

Later I learned that this father-son relationship had been strained for many years. (That is partly why they were sitting on opposite sides of the room.) What counseling, Sunday services, and the urging of friends had not been able to accomplish, the Spirit had resolved in a PRAYzing! moment. Their testimony the next day moved us all to tears.

The stories continued to surface for weeks afterward of other men who pursued reconciliation with their dads or sons after that summit. God had done a truly supernatural work of conviction, grace, and forgiveness.

Through our seemingly inadvertent sputtering start of an afternoon session, the Spirit of God moved mightily to bring about what He knew He needed to accomplish. It was a lesson in humility and sensitivity. Even when a scripted song interrupts our "no agenda" ideal, the Holy Spirit transcends the forms of man to change the hearts of men, if only we can be sensitive to His leading.

V

VISION AND PROVISION

Then I said to them, "You see the distress that we are in,
how Jerusalem lies waste, and its gates are burned with
fire. Come and let us build the wall of Jerusalem, that we
may no longer be a reproach." And I told them of the hand
of my God which had been good upon me, and also of the
king's words that he had spoken to me. So they said, "Let
us rise up and build." Then they set their hands to this
good work.
(NEHEMIAH 2:17-18)

At Grace Church of Eden Prairie, where I currently pastor, 25 percent
of our annual church income is given during the month of December.
Most of that comes in the last week of the year. It is a phenomenon
unique to this community and, frankly, one that has aged me rapidly.
As you might guess, December has become a month of intense anxiety
but also of intentional prayer as we wait on the Lord to provide for His
work through His people.

In this past year, we started a Sunday night prayer and fasting focus

during the final two months of the year. We hosted an hour of intercession lasting from 5:30 to 6:30 p.m., followed by the encouragement
to fast from sundown to sundown, concluding Monday evening. Our
focus centered on the selection of new elders (see Acts 14:23) and the
financial needs of the church.

One Sunday evening during this prayer time, we turned to
Nehemiah 1:1–2:18. Rotating the assignments, we read the passage. I
selected this faith-building passage because it contained the components
of an impossible task, intense prayer, availability to the call of God, deep
brokenness, and spiritual vision.

As I so often do, I asked us to spend the initial time focusing on
what we see about God and His character in the passage. In a wonderful season of praise and worship, we adored God for His many attributes that appeared in the passage. This included spontaneous songs
and many personal reflections of worship in prayer.

Then, in relating to Nehemiah's heart and his experience in review-
ing the devastation of the walls of Jerusalem, we asked the Lord to let
us see the deep needs and brokenness of the world around us, including
our own community and even within the church. We prayed, "Let my
heart break as I see the devastation and brokenness of (blank)." The
Spirit used this season to open our hearts to His view of our church and
neighboring communities.

In the final season of prayer, we considered the challenge issued in
Nehemiah 2:17 and took a moment to let our hearts sense the call of
God to each one. I encouraged each participant to pray, "Lord, just as
Nehemiah had a vision to rebuild the walls, I ask for a greater vision to
(blank)." After each person prayed, the group echoed, "Let us rise up
and build."

As simple as the exercise seemed to be at the moment, the Lord
stirred up fresh vision for ministry, evangelism, prayer, and missions.
We all sensed the need to encourage, pray for, and support the ministry
burdens that were surfacing that night. Indeed, we all desired to rise up

and build for the glory of God.

In the weeks to come, we experienced a new energy in our church services. The Lord orchestrated the selection of some profoundly godly elders. While it had been a tough financial season, we saw the largest surge of giving in the final week of the year witnessed in the history of the church. Additionally, the per capita giving among the congregation was the highest that December than we had ever seen. The Lord is good and faithful in calling us to pray so that we might recognize His good hand and give Him the glory for the vision He births in our hearts.

WORTHY OF MY . . .

Then I looked, and I heard the voice of many angels around
the throne, the living creatures, and the elders; and the
number of them was ten thousand times ten thousand, and
thousands of thousands, saying with a loud voice:
"Worthy is the Lamb who was slain
To receive power and riches and wisdom,
And strength and honor and glory and blessing!"
(REVELATION 5:11-12)

I will call upon the LORD, who is worthy to be praised;
So shall I be saved from my enemies.
(PSALM 18:3)

Years ago, experts believed it was not feasible for local churches to sponsor three-day prayer summits. Part of the rationale was that it required too high a commitment for the average church attendee. They were right and wrong. They were right about the high commitment required. However, by the grace of God, His people can rise to the occasion.

At the time of this writing, I have witnessed thirty-seven local church prayer summits. It is quite a miracle in the sense that individuals have to use vacation time to attend. Hosting a summit at a retreat center for three days can be quite expensive for participants. It involves travel and time away from family. Yet where God calls, He empowers.

At the opening session of a summit early in my ministry, I noticed the participants seemed a bit tired. Many stories circulated about all the sacrifices people had made to come and sit in a room with no speaker, no musical artists, no recreation, and no entertainment—only the presence of God.

As we worshiped, I noticed a theme of the worthiness of God in the songs and Scripture readings. I often say, "The only enduring motive for prayer is that God is worthy to be sought." At this moment, I sensed a vital opportunity to focus our prayers on that idea as an encouragement to the hearts of the participants.

I spoke up and expressed my deep gratitude for the price everyone had paid in order to participate. I reminded the group that all of our sacrifices can serve as an offering to our Lord—one of which He is worthy. Then I asked them to think of all the time, energy, and effort that led to this moment. Next I encouraged the men and women to express to the Lord how worthy He is of all our sacrifices.

People began to pray, finishing the sentence, "Lord, You are worthy of . . ." I was so blessed by this sacrifice of praise. The expressions were diverse and sincere:

"Lord, You are worthy of my vacation time."

"Lord, You are worthy of the time away from my children."

"Lord, You are worthy of my undivided attention."

"Lord, You are worthy of the sacrifice my spouse is making while I am here."

"Lord, You are worthy of every gallon of gasoline expended by every car."

"Lord, You are worthy of my time during these three days."

"Lord, You are worthy of my obedience."

As we prayed and rejoiced, our sacrifices seemed so miniscule compared to the worthiness of God. This experience really set the tone for the entire retreat. The idea has stayed with me and enabled me to adjust my attitude Godward anytime I feel I am paying too high a price in my service for Christ.

X

THE EXchange

But what things were gain to me, these I have counted
loss for Christ. Yet indeed I also count all things loss for
the excellence of the knowledge of Christ Jesus my Lord,
for whom I have suffered the loss of all things, and count
them as rubbish, that I may gain Christ and be found in Him,
not having my own righteousness, which is from the law,
but that which is through faith in Christ, the righteousness
which is from God by faith; that I may know Him and
the power of His resurrection, and the fellowship of His
sufferings, being conformed to His death, if, by any means, I
may attain to the resurrection from the dead.
(PHILIPPIANS 3:7-11)

For I am already being poured out as a drink offering,
and the time of my departure is at hand. I have fought the
good fight, I have finished the race, I have kept the faith.
Finally, there is laid up for me the crown of righteousness,
which the Lord, the righteous Judge, will give to me on
that Day, and not to me only but also to all who have loved
His appearing.
(2 TIMOTHY 4:6-8)

A handful of men gathered for our regular weekly prayer time. As always, we began with Scripture and an open season of worship. After a few minutes, one of the men read from Paul's words in Philippians about the desire to count everything he valued as "loss" for the sake of Christ (see Philippians 3:7). He went on to offer his life and all it entailed for the sake of knowing the Lord.

A few minutes later, another brother read a similar passage from 2 Timothy, again praying about his desire to exchange the things he values in this life for the greater rewards available to him in Christ.

Life is full of trade-offs. I liked the trade-off I was hearing in this prayer time. A creative prayer approach came to my mind as a point of focus for these men.

We prayerfully reread these two passages, and then I asked the men to pray this way: "Lord, I want to exchange the (blank) of my life for the ultimate treasure of (blank) that You offer me in Christ." I encouraged them to think of the things they value but to consider the greater rewards of total surrender to the Savior.

The men opened their hearts to the Lord and one another, offering many aspects of their families, careers, hopes, ambitions, plans, reputations, finances, time, health, hobbies, and inner desires to Christ. With joy, they affirmed the ultimate pleasure of Christ's blessing and eternal reward.

Songs interspersed these prayers of joyful surrender. The focus gripped our hearts so deeply we never got to the normal time of praying for the men of the church and our ministry. Yet we all knew we had found the Lord's agenda for the day. In the end, that is all that mattered. We knew that if we could continue to make this kind of spiritual exchange, the Lord would take care of the rest.

"YES!" AND "AMEN!"

His divine power has given to us all things that pertain to
life and godliness, through the knowledge of Him who called
us by glory and virtue, by which have been given to us
exceedingly great and precious promises, that through these
you may be partakers of the divine nature, having escaped
the corruption that is in the world through lust.
(2 PETER 1:3-4)

For all the promises of God in Him are Yes, and in Him
Amen, to the glory of God through us.
(2 CORINTHIANS 1:20)

Rather than "standing on the promises," many Christians are simply
"sitting on the premises." No one was sitting apathetically at a recent
prayer summit where the Lord captured our imagination with the
wonder of His many assurances to us.

It was the final evening of another three-day summit. The next day
at noon, everyone would head home with the spiritual joy and practical
equipping they had received in our time together. Typically, the final

evening of a summit is comprised of an extended time of Communion. Yet this night, we started with some open-ended, freestyle worship.

Before long, a sister read 1 Peter 1:3-4, extolling the exceedingly great and precious promises that empower us in our participation in His divine nature. Then a brother read 2 Corinthians 1:20, which states that all God's promises are "Yes" and "Amen" in Christ. Indeed, Christ is the affirmation and personification of the promises of God.

I immediately felt the prompting to a moment of PRAYzing! I asked everyone to find specific promises in the Bible. I said that in a moment we were going to simply enjoy a "word-fest" as we heard the promises of God's Word read aloud. Then I offered this instruction: "After each promise is read, I want to ask the men to affirm that promise with a loud 'yes' followed by all the women declaring the 'amen.'" I noted that our response was the announcement that because of Christ, these promises are real and powerful in our lives.

The readings began. Promise after promise flowed from the pages of Scripture, across the lips of many readers, and into hearts that shouted, "Yes!" (men) and "Amen!" (women). The joy and hope were palpable.

Eventually, we had to stop to allow time for our Communion celebration. Clearly, the vast promises of Scripture could have kept us occupied all night.

That evening, our ninety-minute communion service was one of the richest ever, as we all sensed a fresh appreciation for the finished work of Jesus Christ that made God's promises to us powerful and relevant in our lives.

Z

ZIMBABWE AND BEYOND

Behold, the nations are as a drop in a bucket,
And are counted as the small dust on the scales;
Look, He lifts up the isles as a very little thing. . . .
It is He who sits above the circle of the earth,
And its inhabitants are like grasshoppers,
Who stretches out the heavens like a curtain,
And spreads them out like a tent to dwell in.
He brings the princes to nothing;
He makes the judges of the earth useless.
(ISAIAH 40:15,22-23)

For the kingdom is the LORD's,
And He rules over the nations.
(PSALM 22:28)

A couple hundred people from our church gathered on a Sunday evening for what we thought would be a typical "Fresh Encounter" prayer service. I planned the service around the theme of the sovereignty of God from the book of Isaiah. With a foundation of worship about God's dominion and power, we focused on His sovereignty over His people (see 40:10-11), the nations (see 40:12-26), and our individual lives (see 40:27-31).

The reflection on Isaiah 40:12-26 was followed by some songs. As we repeatedly sang the chorus of "Awesome God," we felt a crescendo of energy and celebration. Spontaneously, I sensed it would be appropriate to declare corporately His reign over the nations of the world.[1]

I instructed the participants to think about some of those nations. Of course, the eyes of the world are on the Middle East. Our church has launched special ministry initiatives in certain countries. Perhaps an individual had a particular burden for a region based on a previous mission trip or vacation. Maybe they had friends or relatives in a certain part of the world.

I invited everyone to participate with the thought, *Lord, I declare Your reign over (country name)*. I asked those who felt prompted to announce the name of a particular country, one after another.

Suddenly, earnest declarations filled the room. "Zimbabwe!" "Israel!" "Iraq!" "Iran!" "Brazil!" "Canada!" "Vietnam!" "Russia!" "France!" "The United States!" "Uganda!" "China!" "India!" "Great Britain!" "Egypt!" "Lebanon!" The spontaneous declarations continued for five minutes. Some nations were repeated multiple times. Each cry was filled with compassion. Some were uttered with tears from a broken heart.

My imagination was stimulated with this fresh and dramatic realization of the enormity of the earth and its 6.6 billion residents.[1] The unique troubles and concerns of each nation overpowered me. The overwhelming spiritual needs burdened my heart. Yet the power of God's sovereignty moved me more deeply, stimulating a sense of peace and joyful worship. It was a profound moment!

As the declarations subsided, we repeated the chorus, "Our God is an awesome God! He reigns from heaven above with wisdom, power, and love — our God is an awesome God!" After three rounds, the room spontaneously broke into a standing ovation for our infinite and supreme King reigning over all the earth.

We transitioned to the next season of united prayer, focused on God's sovereignty over our lives and families. Dynamic confidence and trusting joy filled our hearts.

Since He is so powerful over the nations, certainly He can exercise His control and loving care over our individual concerns.

A 4/4 EXAMPLE

In chapter 6, we spoke of the 4/4 pattern as a guide to creative prayer. I want to give you an example of how this can work from a sample portion of the Bible and in a spontaneous fashion.

During our "Seek Week" emphasis, we focus our prayers on passages of Scripture that feature the idea of "seeking" the Lord. Of course, various psalms have this emphasis. One particular morning, we chose Matthew 6:19-34 because of the injunction of verse 33. Here is how PRAYzing! happened for us. Honestly, I walked into the prayer meeting with this text in mind but with no prior preparation or forethought. All of this came to us as the Spirit took the Word and directed us. Read the biblical text below and the explanation of our prayer time, and you'll see how beautifully God conducted our experience.

✝ WHO IS GOD?

Matthew 6:19-34

19 "Do not lay up for yourselves treasures on earth, where moth and rust destroy and where thieves break in and steal; 20 but lay up for yourselves

treasures in heaven, where neither moth nor rust destroys and where thieves do not break in and steal. 21 For where your treasure is, there your heart will be also.

22 "The lamp of the body is the eye. If therefore your eye is good, your whole body will be full of light. 23 But if your eye is bad, your whole body will be full of darkness. If therefore the light that is in you is darkness, how great is that darkness!

24 "No one can serve two masters; for either he will hate the one and love the other, or else he will be loyal to the one and despise the other. You cannot serve God and mammon.

25 "Therefore I say to you, do not worry about your life, what you will eat or what you will drink; nor about your body, what you will put on. Is not life more than food and the body more than clothing? 26 Look at the birds of the air, for they neither sow nor reap nor gather into barns; yet your heavenly Father feeds them. Are you not of more value than they? 27 Which of you by worrying can add one cubit to his stature?

28 "So why do you worry about clothing? Consider the lilies of the field, how they grow: they neither toil nor spin; 29 and yet I say to you that even Solomon in all his glory was not arrayed like one of these. 30 Now if God so clothes the grass of the field, which today is, and tomorrow is thrown into the oven, will He not much more clothe you, O you of little faith?

31 "Therefore do not worry, saying, 'What shall we eat?' or 'What shall we drink?' or 'What shall we wear?' 32 For after all these things the Gentiles seek. For your heavenly Father knows that you need all these things. 33 But seek first the kingdom of God and His righteousness, and all these things shall be added to you. 34 Therefore do not worry about tomorrow, for tomorrow will worry about its own things. Sufficient for the day is its own trouble."

Based on our reading of the passage, participants took time to praise God because He is . . .

- The eternal rewarder and preserver of real treasure (verse 20)
- ✓ The One who knows our hearts (verse 21)
- Our Source of light (verses 22-23)
- Our rightful master (verse 24)
- Worthy of our undivided loyalty (verse 24)
- The One who dispels anxiety and worry (verses 25,28,31)
- The provider for His creation (verse 26)
- Our caring and attentive heavenly Father (verse 26)
- The One who ultimately values us (verse 26)
- Creator of beauty—clothes us with beauty (verses 28-30)
- ✓ The One who knows us and our needs (verse 32)
- Lord of an eternal kingdom (verse 33)
- ✓ Fully sufficient for all things (verse 33)
- ✓ Superintends our lives even in and through trouble (verse 34)

Songs that became part of the flow:

"This Is My Father's World," "Enough," "I'd Rather Have Jesus," "Jesus, Lamb of God, Worthy Is Your Name," "Oh Lord, You're Beautiful," "O Worship the King"

↓ HOW SHOULD WE RESPOND?

Based on verses 19-21 and the connection between that which we treasure and the affection of our heart, we spent some time inviting "His kingdom to come and will to be done" with this sentence prayer: "Because You are my Father, I will treasure You above (blank) and make YOU the ultimate affection of my heart." Many people prayed using this simple but specific idea.

Song: "More Precious Than Silver"

← WHAT SHOULD WE PRAY ABOUT?

At this point, I broke the group into huddles of five or six people.

In affirming the repeated commands to turn away from worry, trust the Father, and seek His kingdom purposes, we took some time to confess worry, express our trust in the Father, and pledge our loyalty to His kingdom purposes.

I suggested we use this prayer pattern for the first few minutes: "When I am tempted to worry about (blank), I will trust You, my Father, to provide all that I need because You value me so much."

Then I encouraged the group to shift their focus in order to intercede for others who have specific areas of need, asking God to deliver them from worry and draw them close to the heart of their Father and provider.

We transitioned after a time with the hymn "'Tis So Sweet to Trust in Jesus."

→ WHERE DO WE GO FROM HERE?

In the final segment, we came back together in the larger group. I noted, "This passage tells us that each day contains trouble but that our Father is able to give us daily grace and strength to overcome." I asked participants to pray, one at a time, in faith and recommitment in light of the inevitable troubles. It went like this: "Father, as I face the trouble of (blank) today, I will seek Your kingdom and righteousness first." Everyone echoed with the affirmation, "And all these things shall be added to you." After ten minutes of this, we stood to sing all three verses of "Seek Ye First."

↑ WHO IS GOD?

We concluded by praising God for His power as we sang the song "He Is Able."

NOTES

INTRODUCTION: ENCOUNTERING THE SPIRIT OF CREATIVITY

1. William R. Miller, *Integrating Spirituality into Treatment: Resources for Practitioners* (Washington, DC: American Psychological Associations, 1999), 86.

CHAPTER 1: NO MORE SLEEPY PRAYER MEETINGS

1. Daniel Henderson, *Fresh Encounters: Experiencing Transformation Through United Worship-Based Prayer* (Colorado Springs, CO: NavPress, 2004).

CHAPTER 2: YOUR CREATIVE HEART

1. Herbert Lockyer, *All The Divine Names and Titles of the Bible* (Grand Rapids, MI: Zondervan, 1988), 6.

CHAPTER 3: PRAYING FROM THE CREATIVE WORD

1. Eugene Peterson, *Working the Angles* (Grand Rapids, MI: Eerdmans, 1987), 44, 47.

2. Jonathan Edwards, in Archie Parrish and R. C. Sproul, *The Spirit of Revival: Discovering the Wisdom of Jonathan Edwards* (Wheaton, IL: Crossway, 2000), 93.

CHAPTER 4: PRAYING WITH CREATIVE CONFIDENCE

1. Brennan Manning, *The Ragamuffin Gospel* (Sisters, OR: Multnomah, 2000), 169.

z/ZIMBABWE AND BEYOND

1. http://www.census.gov/main/www/popclock.html; *U.S. Census Bureau, Population Division.*

AUTHOR

DANIEL HENDERSON is founder and president of Strategic Renewal International, which exists to ignite the heart of the church through personal renewal, congregational revival, and leadership restoration. He has been involved in leading creative prayer experiences as a pastor for over twenty-five years. Daniel speaks to thousands each year in churches, leadership conferences, and renewal events across America and internationally.

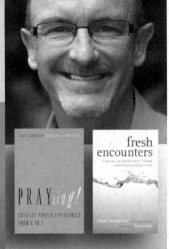

Imagine what God will do when His children pray!

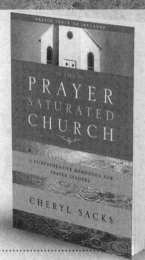

The Prayer-Saturated Church with CD
Cheryl Sacks

Help your church become a house of prayer. Whether you're a pastor, a church prayer-coordinator, or a prayer leader, if you're looking for ways to move your congregation closer to God, this comprehensive prayer handbook will show you how.

978-1-60006-198-1

Accompanied by a CD of printable prayer mobilization guides.

Prayer-Saturated Kids
Cheryl Sacks and Arlyn Lawrence

Whether you are a parent, teacher, or church leader, *Prayer-Saturated Kids* offers you a fresh, faith-filled approach for praying with and for the children in your life. Compelling real life stories combined with creative, reproducible tools will help you teach kids to talk to God and build their faith to become lifelong pray-ers.

978-1-60006-136-3

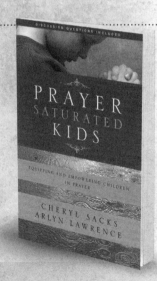

To order copies, call NavPress at **1-800-366-7788** or log on to **www.NavPress.com**.

NAVPRESS

Discipleship Inside Out®

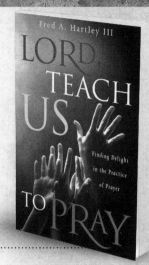

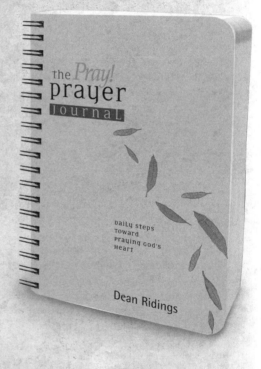